About the Author

Dennis Coath has worked as a presenter, reporter and newsreader with ITV and the BBC. He has co-authored books with England's greatest cricketer, Ian Botham, and most capped footballer, Peter Shilton. He's also written the novel, 'Treat me Like a Dog', about a geriatric rock band. Dennis has interviewed Muhammad Ali, Ayrton Senna, Bjorn Borg, Stanley Matthews, Jonah Lomu and Tyson Fury, among many others. In one year, he reported from Vietnam twice, South Africa, New Zealand, Turkey, France and Italy. Dennis has a B.A. degree in politics and a Master's in history.

Rats, Pies and Pigeon Poo

To Emma the 'Help the Aged Gym Instructor'

Dennis Coath

Rats, Pies and Pigeon Poo

Olympia Publishers
London

www.olympiapublishers.com
OLYMPIA PAPERBACK EDITION

Copyright © Dennis Coath 2023

The right of Dennis Coath to be identified as author of this work has been asserted in accordance with sections 77 and 78 of the Copyright, Designs and Patents Act 1988.

All Rights Reserved

No reproduction, copy or transmission of this publication may be made without written permission.
No paragraph of this publication may be reproduced, copied or transmitted save with the written permission of the publisher, or in accordance with the provisions of the Copyright Act 1956 (as amended).

Any person who commits any unauthorised act in relation to this publication may be liable to criminal prosecution and civil claims for damage.

A CIP catalogue record for this title is available from the British Library.

ISBN: 978-1-80074-848-4

First Published in 2023

Olympia Publishers
Tallis House
2 Tallis Street
London
EC4Y 0AB

Printed in Great Britain

Dedication

I dedicate this book to my wonderful wife, Lisa.

Acknowledgements

Thanks to my wife, Lisa, for her encouragement and editing work. Also, thanks to Steve Lambden for his valuable advice.

Cartoons by Jim Crawley

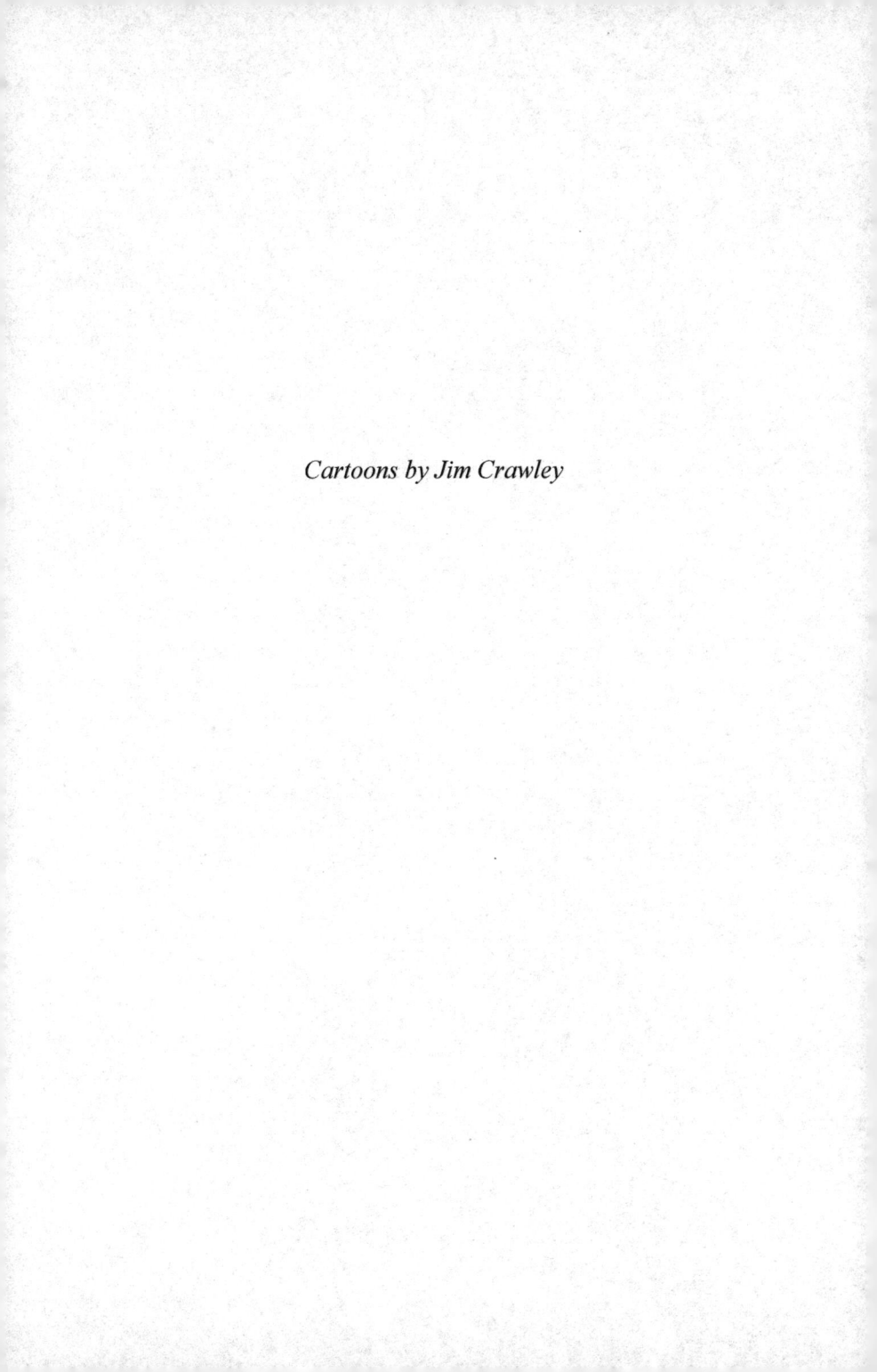

Contents

Sporting Chance 15
A Brief History of Sport Reporting 59
Economics and Sport 94
How to work a patch 112
Moles, Snouts and Informants 120
Commentary and Lives 125
Personality profile 142
Rolling News 149
The Press Conference 155
I could not do that! 159
Sacred Cows 167
Extras, Gripes and Groans 169
Epilogue 189

Sporting Chance

The ball hits the net with an agreeable zing.
A stump cartwheels out of the ground.
The forwards pile over in a driving maul.
A top spin forehand zips across court.
It's a winner!
Nifty overtaking on the main straight.
That last-gasp dip to hit the tape first.
Whose gloves will be raised in triumph?
They're galloping down to the last fence.
It's a shuddering tackle.
A huge six sails into the sky and over the stand.
They're lining up.
Ready to compete, contest and combat.
Smell the sweat.
Scent the liniment.
Feel the impact, and taste the blood.
That WOW Factor!

It is a glamorous career as a sport reporter. I recall standing in layers of pigeon droppings to report on a football match. Dodging a hail of bricks and cobblestones in Istanbul. Avoiding a fusillade of *full* beer cans hurled at my head by French rugby fans. Facing the militia's machine guns in Bilbao, being severely bitten by a horse and terrified by a big black rat, giant lizard and cobras in Vietnam.

Other forms of journalism, apart from political reporting to a certain extent, do not require the same degree of enthusiasm and fanaticism. Sport journalism is unique. A craft and culture out on its own. A species too! After all, you cannot get too excited about a few pompous government ministers changing places or being dismissed from the cabinet, but you may well be stirred up by a managerial sacking or appointment at the football club you support. To quote the legendary Liverpool football manager Bill Shankly. 'Some people think that football is a matter of life and death, I am very disappointed with that attitude. I can assure you it is much, much more important than that.' Obviously, a complete understatement from Bill Shankly.

I will always remember the great Sir Alex Ferguson, summing up the passion and almost being stumped for words, after Manchester United's two dramatic extra-time goals, as they beat Bayern Munich two-one, to win a memorable 1999 Champions' League.

'I can't believe it. I can't believe it. Football. Bloody Hell!'

It was just a wonderful expulsion of relief on the night of his greatest triumph. You could sense the tension, and no wonder, after that nerve-jangling finish. It completed the incredible treble of FA Cup, Premiership and Champions League. In sport, you nearly always witness some sort of drama, and that drama is spontaneous.

I remember a bit of theatrics and tension at a lower division football club when the board were accused of a bit of sharp practice. To counter this, the club called a press conference to dismiss the damaging rumours and stories. At this point the drama turned into a farce. The chairman, in all his pomp and three-piece pin-stripe, with gold watch chain across waistcoat, addressed the conference. He spouted, 'We completely reject these allegations, and we are determined to catch the alligators.' It seems like his accusers were a bit snappy. More on sporting gaffes later.

In the 1940s, '50s and '60s, when kids were asked what they wanted to be when they grew up. Many replied, 'Wanna be a train driver.' It was a bit of a cliché. But Thomas the Tank Engine and the Flying Scotsman can take a lot of the blame for that.

By the 1970s and after the moon landing and the replacement of steam engines with diesel and electric trains, things had become a little more sophisticated, 'wanna be an astronaut.' 'Wanna be a spaceman'; although there were some precocious, self-possessed youngsters who said, 'wanna be the Prime Minister,' or irksome little swots who uttered, 'wanna be a nuclear scientist.'

Nowadays, it is, 'wanna be a rock star,' or 'wanna be a footballer.' But coming up fast on the rails as a career choice is, 'wanna be a sport reporter or commentator.' Why on earth has this occupation, become a rival to rock and roll and football? Where has this strange ambition come from?

I believe the impetus has sprung from the number of channels pumping out constant sport on the television, with SKY and BT as well as the BBC, ITV, and other outlets, seeing sport as a major audience grabber or source of cash. We now have twenty-four-hour sport on tap. Wonderful isn't it! Young people imagine they are interviewing gold medallists at the Olympics, commentating on the World Cup Final or an Ashes Test Match. There is no doubt about it though, sport journalism is becoming a big attraction or seen as a glamorous occupation. Well, after all, being a footballer or rock star requires a modicum of talent. There is also the fact that many young people do not really fancy working for a living. Fair enough.

There is a bit of a misperception about sport reporters. What makes up a typical sport hack? On the few occasions they are portrayed in plays, sitcoms, films, and books, it is as an outdated caricature. Typical sport scribes were male, middle to old aged, wore a shabby suit and always had a cigarette dangling out of their mouths. Sport writers and broadcasters were adjudged as the renegades of journalism – the extreme fringe. The concept of a crowd of sport reporters being like 'the wild bunch' is wildly wide of the mark.

I am glad to report, anthropological studies have shown this unique tribal species has become more refined over the last few decades, owing very much to an influx of women, young apprentices, and graduates into the ranks. The days of the dyed in the wool, old buffers have evaporated away. There is even a cultural and refined side to sport reporters now. Well almost.

You cannot stand still in sport – as a journalist for many years it is fascinating and sometimes fantastic to look back on old tactics, techniques, equipment and kit. Some old images are simply unimaginable. Was it really like that? There are wonderful pictures of sprinters in the 1930s Olympics digging holes in the track to push off from, as they had not invented starting blocks. They used garden trowels for this minor excavation. Early running shoes had spikes like a thick three-inch nail. Excellent for cinder tracks, but not so good if you got raked!

Old football gear is almost comical. Especially those big clodhopper boots of the fifties with industrial toe caps and lethal leather studs that often had a nail sticking through! Then there was the advent of 'continental shoes' at the end of the fifties, as the big bovver boots went out of fashion. Shin pads were as thick as the New Testament. There was also that museum piece; the old leather ball with a lace in it. It was often coated with dubbin to make it waterproof. The truth was the thick leather panels absorbed water on a wet day. When the ball plummeted down from the heavens, it was a dead weight. The best ploy was to nudge your opponent, pretend to head it and miss. If you made a slight misjudgement and caught the ball on top of the head, it felt as though your skull had caved in, and you were seeing stars for the rest of the match. Sometimes you could head the ancient leather sphere and get a bad gash, that is, if the lace was a bit proud and you caught it across the eyebrow. Another example of what has become football memorabilia is those big square wooden goalposts. They were sometimes about six inches across and could have made a frame for a huge building or replaced a rolled steel joist (RSJ).

Great fun to see old football footage from the sixties and seventies. The fashions were extreme. Players with bubble perms, suit lapels about a yard wide and a kipper tie with a knot the size of a cushion. In the seventies and earlier, there is plenty of cricket archive film displaying batsmen without helmets, tiny bats that look like plywood and those barely protective batting gloves with green rubber spikes. The old Formula One cars that appeared as space vehicles at the time, now look like vintage relics. In rugby, backs were small and fast, forwards were the fat boys – big and slow. Now they are all big and fast! Who has still got one of those wonderful old-fashioned antique leather, rugby scrum hats? In the 1980s, Bjorn Borg beat all-comers with his wooden tennis racket. There were also those ancient golf clubs with hickory shafts former 'greats' used to wield.

Physios were unheard off not so long ago. In most sports the 'trainer', usually an older guy, came on to the field of play with a bucket of cold water and sponge. The panacea for all injuries. He looked like a window cleaner invading the pitch. 'You've got a broken leg. I'll just sponge you down and you'll be consistency. Just run it off.' If you were a bit groggy, the trainer just put the icy water down your neck.

As for a warm-up, for most football teams, not that many years ago, it involved a cup of tea, a couple of woodbines, and maybe kicking and headbutting the toilet door. Although I remember one Watford star of the fifties and sixties, an old school half back called George Catleugh, who usually glugged a couple of pints of Mackeson stout at a nearby pub before strolling to the ground swinging his kit bag. George was very dependable and never had a bad game. So much for modern diets. Many past players had a steak as a pre-match meal, which would not have been digested in time before the kick-off. Now the key factor is a carbohydrate load up, usually with pasta, although porridge is becoming a key sport food, especially with boxers. I was interested to note that as British football clubs have devoured pasta, some Italian clubs have switched to potatoes for pre-match energy.

I mentioned liniment earlier. There are now all kinds of muscle rubs and balms. The traditional liniment was pungent, cleared the nostrils and could have been used as a paint stripper. It smelt like a mix of rancid horse radish and strong alcohol. A changing room in the sixties, seventies and eighties always wreaked of the stuff. An unforgettable aroma and an emetic if you were suffering from a hangover. Modern muscle rubs are usually potions of various herbs and oils. There are some more exotic kinds like Emu Oil and Mussel Oil balm. I remember one physio at a rugby club who used a big drum of standard supermarket vegetable oil for massages. If the players took the field on a searing hot day, after one of his rub downs, they could have been fried alive.

Medical remedies for injured athletes have been inventive over the years. The ice bath has become a regular after-match torture instrument, and some old ideas have resurfaced. One of the most revolutionary is the use of leeches. Some rugby players with cauliflower ears have used the medieval method to reduce the swelling and blood clot. Other weird treatments include massage with a horse's placenta, goat's blood and electric shocks. There are also all kinds of alternative medicine practices. It was not so long ago that any boxer with a facial cut had a slice of raw steak attached to it with a strip of plaster. Consistency seemed to come up with a scientific explanation for the efficaciousness of this treatment.

Football tactics are forever changing. We used to play with two full backs, three half backs and five forwards, believe it or not. It was the famous 'W formation'. Many formations are now the other way around, five defenders, three in midfield and two strikers. Where would we be without the Cruyff-turn (not a road junction in Amsterdam)? The Panenka (not a Polish cake) and the Rabona (not a blackcurrant drink)? Set-ups and tactics are constantly evolving. It is sometimes hard to keep up!

It is crucial to realise that in any sport journalism post, you are not likely to start off covering Premiership football, Formula One or the golf majors. It is a great ambition to aspire to, but in any job, you scale the ladder and may slide down a snake in the process. Getting that first job and a start to your career is the most important move. You may be working for a local paper or radio station, and your glamorous assignments will be reporting on Pugworthy Rovers against Grotthorpe United in the Reinforced Concrete League, bog snorkelling from a local swamp, all-in carpet bowls from the Mecca Dancehall or arm wrestling from the Dog and Duck. Journos start somewhere, and the early days are often the least stressful and most pleasurable.

But it can be an aggravating occupation. One of the major irritations sport journalists face, is many people seem to want your job because every fan of sport is an expert, or thinks they are an expert – it is all part of the sport/journo culture. For example, everyone believes they could run the England team better than the manager. You have heard the chant at your local football club about the manager, 'you don't know what you're doing!' After all, why would he? He has only played Premiership and international football for many years, is a FIFA qualified coach and managed a Premiership club in the past. He also monitors the squad in training every day of the week. They also assert they could write a column or perform a commentary better than you. I always enjoy hearing, for example, the Sunday golfer saying something like, 'Rory McIlroy is doing it all wrong. He needs to do this.' He must be right; after all, he is a twenty-two handicapper at Creaky Buttock Golf Club.

Lord Reith, the former BBC Chairman, came out with his famous dull dictate, in more sombre times, about the BBC having to inform, educate and entertain. It all sounded a little condescending. I suspect the 'entertain' was a bit of an afterthought. In successful sport journalism, we need to ENGAGE, ENTHUSE, ENTERTAIN, ENJOY, INFORM, and maybe even EDUCATE? But above all – HAVE FUN!

So, let's go back to the beginning. I am sure there was a spark that made many back page writers or sport broadcasters want to be the eyes and ears of fans, to give them an enthralling account or fresh insight into an event. What made me want to get so close to the action? I could **smell the sweat, scent the liniment, feel the impact, and taste the blood.**

I remember once quite literally completing the set! I was covering a big boxing bill at the old Wembley Arena, when a stunned fighter in one of the preliminary bouts staggered towards the ropes and jettisoned a torrent of blood, toil, tears, sweat and snot (to paraphrase Churchill) all over me. It was an unwelcome shower. My white shirt looked like a mad butcher's apron. Thank goodness for biological washing powder! Though my silk tie could not be salvaged.

But the big event that fuelled my addiction was on Saturday, 30th August, 1958. Chelsea v Wolves in the old first division. My father took me to the match. We were Watford fans (someone has to do it) but watched Chelsea, Arsenal or Fulham when mighty Watford was away. Sixty-two thousand squeezed into Stamford Bridge. There was an aroma of Bovril, Wagon Wheels, and Percy Dalton's famous roasted peanuts, a delicacy at most London football grounds. It was Wolves the Champions, against a fresh-faced Chelsea side, quaintly nicknamed Drake's ducklings, after their manager, the former Arsenal striker, Ted Drake.

The old man must have done a quick course as a clairvoyant, seen something in the stars or read a missive in the tea leaves at the bottom of his cup. He made this prediction, we were about to see a teenage star called Jimmy Greaves become a sensation. That proved to be quite an underestimation.

It was a beautiful sunny day as the great Billy Wright, the England captain, lead out the Wolves. They were the Champions. A team chock full of internationals. There was an air of arrogance and invincibility about them in their old gold shirts. By comparison, Chelsea appeared like a bunch who had only just stepped up from scuffing a tennis ball around the school playground. They looked almost apologetic; but the grubby-nosed street urchins were to triumph and trounce the gnarled, golden veterans on that balmy afternoon.

Billy Wright and his defenders needed more than a magic sponge, bucket of cold water and cup of tea at full time. Maybe sea-sickness tablets to ease the dizziness might have been more appropriate, as the elusive and impish Greaves sashayed, swayed, swerved, swaggered and side-stepped around them to score FIVE and headline the back page of every Sunday paper. It was the best individual performance I have ever witnessed on a football field. The result – Chelsea 6 Wolves 2.

I can still remember the event as though it was yesterday. What a game. What a day out. What an occasion. What a surprise. What a story. I was ten years old and completely intoxicated by the atmosphere. When I got home, my mother was pestered to sew the Greaves number eight on the back of my football shirt. I recall I did not sleep that night and with my pocket money, bought a few Sunday papers to read the reports of THAT match.

Jimmy Greaves went on to have the best goals per game record as an England striker, an extraordinary forty-four goals in fifty-seven internationals.

Fast-forwarding to 1981, twenty-three years later. An astonishing coincidence! I was sitting in the ATV sports room, where I worked as a reporter, with my Controller of Sport, Billy Wright, and our football expert Jimmy Greaves! It was an extraordinary happening chatting away in an office with two colleagues who were the central figures in the sporting drama which most influenced my life. Not surprisingly, that match in August 1958 was an occasion that Jimmy remembered rather more fondly than Billy. In fact, "Greavsie" still bamboozled everyone with his wit, banter and wonderful anecdotes. Billy and Jimmy enjoyed a great camaraderie.

I have many more tips about how to rub shoulders with the great and good in sport and unearth some original stories. I recall the Chelsea v Wolves match as the first time I had THAT feeling. It is what great sport journalism is all about, **smell the sweat, scent the liniment, feel the impact and taste the blood** – seeping out of the newsprint, radiating from the radio waves or searing and streaming out of the TV screen. **That WOW Factor!**

For me, the best example of a writer who could transport you to a scene, situation or event was the incomparable Hugh McIlvanney in the Observer or Sunday Times, especially with his insight on big boxing matches.

Reading his dispatches was the next best thing to being at ringside or in the training gyms. But McIlvanney was also a brilliant and witty raconteur when covering football or racing. This was his description of a George Best goal.

'George had come in along the goal line from the corner flag in a blur of intricate deception. Having briskly embarrassed

three or four challengers, he drove the ball high into the net with a fierce simplicity that made spectators wonder if the acuteness of the angle had been an optical illusion.'

Again, on George Best... *'feet as sensitive as a pickpocket's hands.'*

A McIlvanney summing up of the harsh weather conditions at Ayr Racecourse... *'It was the kind of wind that seemed to peel the flesh off your bones and come back for the marrow.'*

And on Boxer Joe Bugner... *'The physique of a Greek statue but fewer moves.'*

Just read his account of the fearsome George Foreman in action as World Heavyweight champion... *'The pulverising blows tend to come from both hands in long arcs, sweeping diagonally to his opponent's head, and the vast arms often brush contemptuously through efforts at parrying defence.*

He quarters the ring with a deadly sense of geometry, employing a perfectly timed side-step that cuts off escape routes as emphatically as a road-block.'

When my Sunday paper dropped through the letter box, the first article or column I read was always the latest by the inimitable Hugh McIlvanney.

One of the most important lessons to learn for any aspiring sport journos is *do not copy other writers and broadcasters*, even McIlvanney. Work diligently to examine and evaluate methods and approaches and assimilate ideas from other people but try to develop your own style. There are many different sport broadcasters I enjoy or have enjoyed listening to because of their contrasting techniques. Too many to mention, but here goes.

My favourite commentator of all time is Richie Benaud on cricket. His great strength was his authority and expertise. As a former Australian skipper, the greatest cricket captain I have ever seen, he was ahead of the players on the field in terms of tactical ploys. He had also pursued parallel professions, working as a journalist in Sydney and enjoying a celebrated cricketing career. What I enjoyed about his commentaries was he kept his astute remarks to a pithy minimum. Sky's cricket coverage is admirable, especially with the knowledgeable Michael Holding at the mic, who for me, has become the voice of summer, along with Jonathan Agnew on the BBC Test Match Special. There is nothing better on a long journey than to be able to lessen the grind on the motorway by listening to the dulcet tones of "Aggers" and "TMS". Desmond Lynam was the smoothest act on TV and a very safe pair of hands at the tiller. The treble act of Gary Lineker, Alan Shearer, and Ian Wright on 'Match of the Day', is always informative, thought-provoking and often hilarious. Horse Racing has provided some great voices and commentators. Peter O'Sullevan was for years the voice of the sport, but I have really enjoyed hearing Graham Goode and Derek Thompson.

Other styles that come to mind are the vaudeville, off the wall method of David 'Bumble' Lloyd. The cosy, fireside chat of the late Peter Alliss in golf. The nimbleness and ease of Gabby Logan switching from covering football to rugby or athletics. I used to love the wonderfully combative manner of Eddie Hemmings and Mike Stephenson in Rugby League. There's Sue Barker, a champion on the court and in complete, calm control as a tennis presenter. The excellent voice and clarity of Nick Mullins in Rugby Union and the quick-fire wit and fusillade of wonderful facts and stats from Jeff Stelling on a Saturday afternoon. I also love to hear Dion Dublin on Radio and TV, but especially on *'Homes Under the Hammer'*, one of my guilty pleasures. It is a must to watch on a cold or wintry morning, and Dion has made it almost into a great 'Sporting Event'.

Without doubt, the best all-round writer and broadcaster I have worked with is John Helm at BBC and ITV. It is no exaggeration that John could write or broadcast in individual style on any sport. His knowledge is phenomenal. I once saw him carrying out a cricket commentary and filling in the score book simultaneously. Try it out!

There are so many others I could mention, but all these characters are inspirational. There are a great number of paper scribes I enjoy, like Henry Winter on football, Stephen Jones and Stuart Barnes's opinions on Rugby and Michael Atherton's cricketing insight. Graeme Souness always provides a great read in his insightful Sunday column, and his comments on SKY Football add a lot of depth to the programmes.

To be a sporting journo or broadcaster, it always helps if you are brought up in an atmosphere where sport is a way of life or religion. Footballs in the yard, a netball hoop on the side of the house, wickets drawn on a wall, a badminton net across the lawn, a scrummaging machine in the flowerbed or a punch bag in the shed. Or if you are mega-rich, a golf course, tennis court or racing circuit in the back garden would not go amiss!

My father had me kicking footballs and bowling cricket balls as soon as I was out of the pram. His idea of getting me to appreciate cricket was to bowl a ball as fast as possible, aiming at my ribs. An introduction to facing fast bowlers! As a child, winters were spent playing football on the local recreation ground. Those big brown boots, a Reader's Digest for a shin pad and the fashionable plastic Frido balls. We always had a nucleus of ten to twenty for a game, which may have taken two or three hours and ended 29-27... if it was a low-scoring affair. Then we would trudge home dripping with mud. After the cup final at the beginning of May, we switched to cricket and again wended our way back home after the gladiatorial clash, covered in soil, sweat and grass stains.

This fanaticism continued. In my late teens, I did a spell as a crematorium gardener. While carrying out my grave tasks, I used to smuggle in a bat and ball, and a pal and I played on the crematorium lawn of remembrance. Of course, we played for… 'The Ashes'. Unfortunately, on one afternoon, we had a big one-a-side England v Australia match going at full swing and were concentrating so hard on the game that we did not notice the crematorium superintendent coming round the corner. The finger was wagged. We were both given out, sacked on the spot! The annoying thing was, I was forty-nine not out at the time.

The craziest and most dangerous escapade of sporting lunacy I ever indulged in was as a teenager to gain free admittance to Stamford Bridge. At one time, Chelsea had the second biggest stadium in England. Nearly 83,000 people watched a match against Arsenal in 1935. At one side of the ground, high above the tube, was the big bank, which was built up from thousands of tons of material from the excavation of the Piccadilly line. The bank was often jam-packed with thousands of spectators. A pal of mine and I carried out a daredevil stunt on a couple of occasions. We ran off the end of the platform of Fulham Broadway station and checked there were no trains coming or going before running along the track. There was a very steep slurry bank which we climbed up. It was a case of two steps forward and one back. If you slipped, it could have been a calamitous slither down to the railway track below. On reaching the summit, we were able to scale a fence and drop into the crowd on the bank. The free admission meant we did not have to use our pocket money to see the game.

I am amazed by the number of courses not just in journalism and media studies but specifically in sport that have sprung up at colleges and universities. They are constantly changing. We are getting studies like sport and media and sport and business. Soon it will be sport and nuclear physics, sport with astrochemistry or sport and advanced brain surgery. It is another developing facet of that 'wanna be a sport reporter syndrome'. Young people have become fired up and fixated about becoming a sport journo. With all due respect to excellent college courses, you really start to find out more when you are 'cast into the wild'. As in any job, you must 'do your apprenticeship'. Strive to find any work, even if it is a mundane task at a newspaper office, on radio, television, or social media. You can only work from the inside.

I have friends and colleagues who got into sport journalism, TV and Radio, more by accident than design. One colleague I worked with started by cleaning the toilets at ITV. Another gave up an acting career and somehow evolved into a sport reporter. I can also recall former colleagues who were variously, a solicitor, estate agent, caretaker and monk before re-emerging as reporters on radio and TV stations.

Beware, to be a sport reporter you need hide like a rhinoceros. It is a profession where you cannot become too prissy or sensitive. There will be a lot of disappointments and a few insults thrown in your direction. I remember for an early job as a trainee, the editor saying very flatteringly:

'We will have to send you out on this job, as I cannot get anyone else.' Thanks for the compliment.

You also must be on your toes all the time. Even football managers can display a sharp wit. I once walked into it, when I asked Brian Clough, 'Can I have a couple of words, Brian.' To which he replied, 'Yes, young man… fuck off.' Another manager, when asked for a quick word, retorted, 'velocity, that's a quick word.'

You will always be brought down to earth. I was once doing an outside broadcast about a big snooker match featuring World Champion Steve Davis. The area for the Outside Broadcast (OB) with the snooker table was cordoned-off, and we had two camera crews getting ready for a rehearsal. Suddenly a corpulent woman dressed in a kaftan, that looked like a tent, pushed through the barrier and wagged her finger at me. She said, 'I've seen you on telly and you look really come and get me, but in the flesh, you're a big disappointment.'

The two camera crews were paralysed with laughter. I was worried they would not recover in time for the broadcast. I was still a little bewildered when a skinny young lad pushed through the crowd and led the woman away by the arm shouting out in a loud voice, 'c'mon mum, you're fucking pissed.'

There are many occasions when you are going to face the unpredictable or be caught unawares. I was lucky to enjoy the pioneering days of local radio at the start of my career. It was a bit of a 'sweat shop' and you had to learn very quickly. When I started, there were just eight local stations in the whole of England, all run by the BBC. Now there are hundreds. There was a sense of adventure working at these new centres. I began at Radio Leeds, where we covered a vast area of Yorkshire. As well as Leeds, the editorial area extended to Bradford, Huddersfield, Halifax, Wakefield, Harrogate and York.

The actual radio station was very compact, and there was only one studio for broadcasting. This studio was starting to look a little shabby, and it was decided that it needed a bit of a spruce up. Budgets at the time were very tight. As the only studio could not be put out of action, two decorators were hired and were instructed to carry out their work, but if the red light came on, signifying a live broadcast, they had to keep quiet. As much of the material was recorded on tape, there was plenty of time for the workmen to beaver away. If there was just a short break for an announcement or bulletin, they just paused, often frozen like a statue with brush or roller in hand. When a live programme was carried out, the two men retreated for a lengthy tea break. At first, this system worked very efficiently, until one morning, I came into the studio to read the eleven o'clock news bulletin. I played the news cassette jingle, and before I could read the first story, a loud voice called out. 'Can you pass the putty, Bert?' It was very hard to follow that. I stumbled through the bulletin and came out of the studio to the office, where most of my colleagues were still in fits of laughter, some in a state of collapse over their desks.

In a lot of newspaper offices and on TV and Radio stations, there has been a 'buggin's turn' attitude and approach to sport reporting by some managers and editors. They think, anyone can do it. They cannot! The cooking correspondent, obituary writer or transport reporter may be told to take over as a sport journalist. You can mug up on most subjects, but if you do not have a thorough background in sport, or the required knowledge and passion, you may well struggle.

Without sounding contradictory, someone with wide sporting knowledge, and a feel for the subject, could gain expertise in a specific event they are not particularly familiar with. For example, I was more of a football and cricket man. I knew less than nought about motorcycle racing but was sent to cover the British Grand Prix at Donington Park. I was blown away by the spectacle, the event and the personalities involved; in those days, the wonderfully loquacious Barry Sheene and his American rival Kenny Roberts. Sheene almost acted like 'Mein Host', and if you wanted to interview someone, he would sort it out, as he seemed to be able to converse in a variety of languages. He had a great memory and always recalled the first names of every camera operator, sound technician and electrician in the crews. I made it my business to research the sport thoroughly and ended up covering events at home and abroad.

As Bob the Builder was often quoted, 'can we fix it? yes, we can!' That applies to budding sport journos. If you are asked to cover an event, and you know little about it, you CAN fix it. Do your research and talk to some leading participants or competitors. I have friends who became leading correspondents in certain activities of which they had little prior knowledge, but through hard graft, became the doyens of that sport. By talking to the extraordinary Barry Sheene and other racers like the wonderful 'Rocket' Ron Haslam, I did my apprenticeship in bike racing and was thrilled to watch and report on the likes of Sheene, Wayne Rainey, Kevin Schwantz and Valentino Rossi.

For any sport, you will further your knowledge, find a different perspective and get plenty of good advice by talking to top players, competitors, coaches, and managers. I always liked to listen carefully to what they had to say and picked their brains. Nottingham, at one time, was like an academy for learning about football. What could be better than listening to Brian Clough and Peter Taylor at Forest – surely the best managerial partnership of all time, after taking the unfashionable club to two European Cups? Over the River Trent at Notts County, the mercurial Jimmy Sirrel was in charge, a man who took the famous old club from the fourth to the old first division. Taylor and Sirrel were the two best talent spotters I have ever witnessed.

Peter had this extraordinary ability to identify star players who had veered off the rails a little or were underperforming and get them to sign for Forest. They would then have a resurgence at the City Ground. I once asked Peter about unearthing talented players. He looked at me as though I was daft. He told me it was simple and just looked for one factor. 'Can he play?' I have those three words etched on my mind when I watch footballers. Peter was also keen to delve into the player's backgrounds very thoroughly to check any new signing was not going to be burdened with off-the-field problems that may affect his form. It was very shrewd management.

Jimmy Sirrel was also an extraordinary recruitment officer. He picked up a string of bargain buys and developed star material from the youth team. Jimmy's judgement of a player was acute. I recall there was a striker with a second division club who was attracting the top scouts and linked with first division clubs, including Notts County. I enquired if Jimmy fancied signing the player, and he said that he had watched him and dismissed the lad, as he claimed was lacking in a bit of courage. When I watched him, I realised that Jimmy was spot on. The player did not relish heavy challenges and was not keen on putting himself about. In old-fashioned parlance, he was 'a goal hanger'. I observed the player gradually sank down the leagues; he scored goals but never established a place at a club. Behind a bluff and tough Glaswegian exterior, Jimmy was a kind man who always found time to chat. One day he explained how his four-two-four system worked by utilising salt and pepper pots, drink, and sauce bottles. They were lined up like chess pieces on his office table. There could have been the tomato ketchup gambit or checkmate with beer bottle and salt cellar. It was a brilliant analysis and like getting an advanced lecture on football tactics.

I gained a lot of knowledge on goalkeeping by writing two books with Peter Shilton. With 125 England appearances, and it should have been more, Peter is England's most capped footballer. He played in the international side for twenty years and took part in more than a thousand league matches. I find it strange that when pundits talk about our greatest players, Peter is rarely mentioned. It is as though goalies do not count. He would certainly be included in my top six England stars of all time. Peter's insight, knowledge and attention to detail is extraordinarily thorough. He is very articulate and could virtually dictate out chapters for the books.

When I watch keepers, I always look for the guidelines that Peter explained so clearly.

Sport reporters are an elite club. As I hinted earlier, they are usually a fanatical, unrelenting band of brigands set apart. The collective noun would be a 'ruck' of sport reporters or maybe a 'raiding party'. It is fair to say that news reporters, with the required knowledge, who manage to make the big transfer into sport, recognise they have joined a whole 'new culture'. I remember one top news journalist who moved into sport saying on his first day in the new job that he was bewildered.

The traditional atmosphere in a 'sports room' can be a bit

wild and wacky. It is the lunatic fringe. In slack times reporters usually devise interesting and inventive expenses, but at one office we used to let off steam by throwing an ice hockey puck around, playing a short form of cricket on the carpet or hiding each other's mobile phones, often by taping them to the roof. Little things! Why is the culture of sport reporting so different?

That is because it is a very demanding trade to use a sweeping generalisation. **People watch news as a DUTY. They watch sport as a MUST.** Viewers and listeners do not tune into news bulletins to see if there has been a rise in unemployment or a banana shortage, but they will watch sport for a specific purpose, to find out a result, or perhaps a piece of transfer news. In my opinion, general news often just reacts to stories, sport news is creative and can set the agenda. When you need to produce some sport stories, you can often trigger a reaction. Fans have a feeding frenzy for the latest news, like a peckish posse of

Great White Sharks, who have missed out on a tuna butty for breakfast.

The fascination stems from a starting point; most of the stories are about people. In any pub, café or workplace, sport is the main topic of conversation above any other subject, even politics. I remember slogging away on a building site near the War Office in London, where some of the workers used to upturn a dustbin lid over a coke brazier, melt a block of lard in the makeshift pan and fry dozens of eggs. They would then sit around on piles of bricks, eat egg sarnies and pull out a newspaper. Everyone would start by reading the sport pages. Or, to be more accurate, they would only read the back pages. For a few minutes, there would be a line of brickies and labourers reading the sport stories, dripping egg yolk all over their papers and overalls and slurping huge enamel mugs of tea. After scanning the sport, a vigorous discussion would start, usually about football. They were mainly Arsenal, Spurs and Chelsea fans. The conversation was quite animated. They really let off a bit of verbal steam. As a Watford fan, I was considered an outcast or eccentric and did not get a word in.

Sport conjures up many different and conflicting opinions and often headstrong views. For most, though, it is a form of escapism. If your team wins a trophy, if your horse romps home at fifty to one, or if your favourite performer wins an Olympic gold medal, a feeling of complete euphoria sets in.

Sport also mirrors life with its trials and tribulations, and supporting a football club is the ultimate in religious fervour. After all, fewer than five per cent of the population are churchgoers. It has been estimated that around half the people of Britain support a soccer club. Karl Marx once stated that religion was the opiate of the masses, now, it is sport. It could be construed that Lenin, a follower of Marx, started the trend. He was an avowed atheist, a left-winger, and a fanatical supporter of the club Zorya Luhansk and even ordered the building of their first stadium.

It is commonplace for a chat about sport to be 'the icebreaker', especially in business meetings. Before any serious talks about a takeover or company transaction, the conversation will be, 'I saw your lads did well winning away on Saturday' and 'how's your new manager making out?' After a bit of essential football chat, it will be down to boring business. 'For god's sake, let's get this damn tedious deal done and then we can talk football again.'

There are many other reasons why sport is all-consuming. People take sides and are usually very biased and partisan. There is a great degree of civic honour involved; communities take a great pride in their team. For fans, there is a love of the detail, minutiae and those nerdy, absorbing statistics. Great to bore people with, in the pub or at parties.

Sport also provides many long strung-out affairs. These prove to be addictive, ongoing sagas. Stories tend to be less clear-cut as there are so many different nuances and ideas and so much fervour aroused. Sport sagas can last longer than the Wars of the Roses and become more complex. There is almost a sense of desperation; sport fans want to read or listen to something about their football club, rugby side, the state of the Formula One season, etc. This has helped the boom in social media. I met one Man U fan who had different whistles and bells on his mobile to signify new info coming up on a vast multitude of websites and feeds. He was accompanied by a series of startling sounds emanating from the phone in his pocket every few minutes.

People want to lap up all the details. To use two similar-sized cities as examples, around 30,000 might watch Leicester City or Nottingham Forest, but I will guarantee that more than half the population of approximately 300,000 in each City will know all about the goings-on at the football clubs, even if they have never watched a game in their lives. It is quite a strange aspect of sport, that people who profess to have little interest will have a fair idea of what is going on and proffer an opinion.

In a sport department I worked at, we used to have a cliché, if we appointed a new journalist or reporter they had to have 'done the hard yards'. That is, toiled for an organisation and spent plenty of numbing, boring hours hanging around in dank corridors at football grounds, watched unending training sessions on freezing cold winter days, attended some very dull four-day County Championship cricket matches or had mud and manure kicked in their faces while studying racehorses on the gallops. In job interviews, we often asked a candidate who was the left back for... Mansfield Town, Bristol Rovers or Exeter City? If they knew, they were either very sad or had a fanatical sporting knowledge. Yes, it could pay to be a sporting nerd or anorak.

As a general news journalist, you are often an expert on a topic for a day. The editor may cajole a reporter into covering anything from a drop in car manufacturing output, to a discovery of a Saxon treasure, to a rise in the cost of cauliflowers. Which reminds me, I once worked for an editor who had a vegetable fetish. 'We must cover this story about the giant marrow that is bigger than an intercontinental ballistic missile.' 'This is a great tale about a turnip with a face like Jesus.' I digress a little, but with the help of the ever-expanding net, it is a lot easier to research a story and become relatively well informed in no time at all. You can often get away with a minor error in a news report. In sport, the slightest gaffe tends to ruin a reporter's credibility.

I have read, heard, and seen many sporting shockers. My favourite was a radio presenter reading out a tennis score and announcing, 'Borg beat McEnroe 6 minus 3, 6 minus 4.' I enjoyed a golf story about the great Steve Ballesteros. A rugby report about the Leicester Tigers *eleven* – my word, they must have struggled. One manager told me they had a great harmonium in the dressing room. I wonder who played it! A footy commentator once said, 'I was saying the other day how often the most vulnerable area for goalies is between their legs.' But best of all, a letter sent from a sport department to our great former Olympic Champion and 2012 Olympic supremo… Sir Bastian Coe!

I remember after a four-nil defeat, a football manager saying, 'we wuz the better side until they scored.' I replied, 'but they scored after four minutes!'

Even doyens of sport can emit extraordinary blunders. John Snagge was established as the voice of the annual University boat race on the Thames. Commentating on the contest on BBC Radio in 1949, Snagge's accurate description was, 'I can't tell who is leading – it's either Oxford or Cambridge.' More great sporting slip-ups later in the chapter on commentaries!

But hearing a few sporting gems rather than gaffes can be even more memorable. Before big contests, boxing provides great quotes and trash talk. The best inevitably came from Muhammad Ali.

'I've seen George Foreman shadow boxing, and the shadow won.'

'He's (Sonny Liston) too ugly to be the world champ. The world champ should be pretty like me.'

'It's just a job. Grass grows, birds fly, waves pound the sand. I beat people up.'

And on his forthcoming contest against Joe Frazier in the Philippines. 'It's gonna be a chiller and a killer and a thriller, when I fight the gorilla in Manila.'

The point must be underlined again, to fans and supporters, sport really is like a religion, but the worshippers are more devout. If you make a big mistake as a sport reporter, it will take time for your gaffe to be consigned to the file marked... 'forgotten'. You must know your stuff and do your homework.

I remember a press conference at Southwell Racecourse more than twenty-five years ago. It was the trial of one of the first all-weather tracks in Britain. The story attracted an uncommon amount of interest. No less than a dozen camera crews, some from abroad, radio reporters and many newspaper writers turned up for the press day. To sample the new surface, the renowned, eight times, Champion Jockey Peter Scudamore galloped up and down a few times and then dismounted and walked over to the rails to address the battalion of the press. Peter expertly and politely fielded questions like, 'what was it like to ride on the surface?' 'Was there much kick back?' 'Is it faster or slower than turf?' After patiently replying to a host of questions, there was a pause, and a young radio reporter with a tape recorder yelled out – 'Peter!' Scudamore replied, 'yes'. The reporter very earnestly inquired, 'What is your second name?' The press gathering dissolved into laughter; the reporter was not too well informed. At the very least, you should know the name of the person you are interviewing!

Another incident of a young journo being not too familiar with a sport was a situation at the final whistle of a Premiership football match. The reporter was detailed to get an interview with the goalie. The awkward fact was the young person was not too sure which one was the goalkeeper. In the end, the journo confronted one of the players and said, 'excuse me, but I'm looking for the goalkeeper.' The player, the only one in an individual number one jersey, held up his hands with the big gloves on and said, 'will I do?'

There are three vital factors that need to be put into the mix, before you start a career as a sport journo – contacts, angles and imagination. The very first task is to start a personal contact file, both electronically and in an address book. If you see Lionel Messi in Tesco, Serena Williams in the chippie, Lewis Hamilton in the dry cleaners, or Ronaldo in Poundland, try to obtain their mobile numbers. A journalist is often only as good as his or her contacts, and you build up a network over a career. It is important to get to know and fraternise with influential people and build up their trust. A prized mobile number can often lead to a big story. 'Hi Lionel, how's it going, mate?' 'Sssshhh, I'm just on the line to Cristiano!'

Reporters always talk about angles for stories. This is not advanced geometry. Anyone with half a brain cell can work it out – even a sport journo. Ask yourself, what is the most important or fascinating aspect or angle for the story? This is usually obvious. You do not need a double first in nuclear physics and existential psychiatry to work it out. Few sport reporters have these qualifications. This story is all about… the hat trick scorer who won the cup final, Lewis Hamilton guiding his car to victory on the last lap with a shredded tyre and the horse that won the Grand National at a hundred to one. But by delving a little deeper, doing your research, chatting to people and being patient, it is possible to unearth some less obvious but just as interesting tales. This is where your imagination comes into play.

I was once talking to a horse racing trainer just before a meeting. It was a dull summer's day at the height of the silly season of July and August. There was absolutely nothing going on. So I decided to head down for an afternoon at the races. I was searching for a story, a hint of a story, any story, any bloody story, please God, find me a story! A race meeting is the best place to be when you are searching for a tale or two. There is usually something going down with horses, jockeys, trainers and owners. The trainer rather casually told me his mare, which was ten months pregnant, was going for her third win in a row. Apparently, the expectant mum seemed to get faster as the weeks went on and just loved running. The horse, which looked very bulky, duly completed the trio of victories. Given that the gestation period for a horse is eleven to twelve months, this was quite an extraordinary feat. It made a wonderful off-beat story with extensive national coverage. The heavily pregnant horse that kept running and winning!

My favourite tale happened during the miners' strike in

1984. A young man phoned the office late in the day as I was turning out the lights and about to head for home. He started blurting out loads of facts about his motorbike. He had added a Volvo truck turbo charger, an aluminium whatsit, a super thing-me-jig and bored the engine out. He was starting to bore me out. I just wanted to go home. He continued with lots of techno talk, and I was about to make an excuse and put the phone down. This didn't seem to be going anywhere.

In a final attempt to unravel an angle to the story and decipher what this was all about. I asked him, 'what does the bike actually do?' I then established he had the fastest road bike in the world. Nought to sixty in a flash! Now we were getting somewhere! This was really something else. I was starting to become interested in the story. I then enquired about what he did for a living. The answer… 'I'm a miner.' This was at the height of the pit workers' action. Some were still going about their business in the collieries, the majority were out. He told me he was working. Next question, 'how do you get to work?' 'On my bike!' It was a big national story – **the man who rode through the picket lines on the world's fastest bike**. The machine was quite simply like a rocket on two mega tyres and street legal. Watching the bike quite literally take-off from the traffic lights was amazing. I felt that my car alongside was standing still. It is the unusual story that you exclusively break, owing to your own initiative or luck, that is always the most satisfying.

Persistence is another important tool of the trade, but it is a difficult balance to achieve because you must be dogged and determined without irritating the hell out of people. On the 1998 England rugby tour of New Zealand, all the broadcasters and writers were trying to get an exclusive interview with the incomparable Jonah Lomu, the giant six-foot-five winger with an

Olympic sprinter's pace, who trampled England underfoot in the World Cup. At the time, he was just about the biggest personality in sport, let alone rugby.

The New Zealand rugby officials were not being very accommodating. Everyone wanted that big chat with Lomu and the authorities just did not want to play ball. I chipped away over a few days by talking to other All Black players and their management and press officers. Eventually, and probably to shut me up, I was granted a couple of minutes for a snatched interview standing up. But I had prepared an anteroom at the training facility with two nice armchairs and half guided, and half shoved the nineteen stone goliath into our makeshift interview studio. The New Zealand press officer tried to stop us, but Jonah, a gentleman giant, was happy to do the chat. We sat down and got the interview whirring away before the official could intervene. Afterwards, the press officer was furious and snapped, 'that wasn't allowed, mate!' Too late, mate, we had recorded an interview with the legendary Jonah, who was very pleasant and forthcoming.

I once had a rather tedious quest in trying to get an interview with Ayrton Senna, who some critics say is the greatest racing driver in history. Second to Lewis Hamilton, in my opinion. At the time I felt it would have been easier to facilitate a chat with the Queen, Lord Lucan, Elvis Presley or Boris Yeltsin. Senna was surrounded by his team and close advisors; it was like trying to gate crash a tight-knit syndicate, like a pensioner's dominoes club. It was certainly difficult to make contact or get near to the Brazilian star. Eventually, after a lot of pondering, with half the day gone by, I found a 'way in'. At the nearby café, while taking a coffee break, desperation was setting in. I started to talk to one of the mechanics and noticed from his overalls that he was in

'Senna's Team'. We had a good chat, and I found out he was part of the driver's inner circle. The man, who got on very well with Ayrton, acted as a go-between. Two hours later, he managed to persuade the F1 ace to do a chat. He was a little reticent at first. I was not sure if he was arrogant or shy. People told me it was probably the latter. But I had grabbed the interview I had been seeking and was grateful to my mediator.

While at ITV, I enjoyed a good working relationship with the extremely talented Carl Froch, who became World Super-middleweight Boxing Champion. As well as being a super-athlete, Carl is a very bright guy with interests in business and property. He is now doing a lot of work as a TV boxing analyst, and I could see him forging a career as an actor.

When he was training to fight for the World Crown against John Pascal of Canada, a formidable opponent, Carl and his team set up an out-of-the-way training base in the wilds of County Mayo in Ireland. I was indebted to them when they agreed I would be the sole journalist in the camp.

My camera operator, one of the staff and I wanted to try out the Guinness at a nearby hostelry. Carl even acted as chauffeur and drove us there and back. He watched on in envy as we sampled a perfect pint of the smooth black stout. I went on a morning run with Carl and some other boxers but soon lagged well behind as they disappeared faraway into the distance. I even had a go on the pads and sampled the fast hands of a man about to become a World Champion; the power was awesome – and he was pulling his punches! The routine under the eye of expert trainer Rob McCracken was formidable; that early morning run was followed by gym work and then sparring. Squeezed in between was time for meals. Our week's work provided a series of TV features as a preview to Carl's victory in the big fight and capture of the WBC World Championship belt. He was very helpful and forthcoming. Once again, you need contacts to establish trust, to break a lot of stories and get the chance to cover events.

I am forever in debt to that great scholar and gentleman David Gower, the most natural and elegant batsman I have ever seen. After his cricket career, his eloquence and personality led to him becoming a top presenter and commentator. David was always a joy to interview and very entertaining. I remember a time when he was high on the agenda of national news and sport stories for the day. Gower was adjudged to have made some sort of misdemeanour by the puritanical cricketing authorities. For the journos, it was a 'no lose' situation. If he was dropped from the England team, it was a big story. If he was retained, it was also a big story.

I arranged to go round to Gower's house to grab an interview just after the expected announcement. When I arrived, I asked him, what the outcome was, but he did not know. The decision had been delayed. The clock was ticking around fast towards the lunchtime bulletins. I was thinking, 'what am I going to do?' when Gower volunteered that he would carry out two interviews, one pretending he had been left out, another voicing his joy at being reselected. So, he began the first chat with a comment like 'I am devastated to be left out of the team.' And began the second with a line like… 'I am delighted to be included in the England side.' It was a quite masterful performance. He should have been Oscar-nominated. The two interviews went back to the studio, and Gower was sadly dropped from the line-up. The correct interview was broadcast, and the other erased. I really could have stitched David up, but I was indebted to him and delighted that he had come to my aid. Hopefully, I had gained his trust, but he had saved the day.

There is another factor in sport reporting, in fact, all journalism, of course: sheer luck! But it is often a combination of fortune allied with hard graft. As in many walks of life, I believe if you work hard, you make your own luck. One of my favourite journalists of all time was ITN's legendary Michael Nicholson. Nicholson sent back dispatches from eighteen war zones. He covered the fall of Saigon in the Vietnam war and reported on the Falklands war. But Nicholson's most famous scoop was during the Turkish invasion of Cyprus in July 1974. He and his camera team were positioned in a field with Turkish paratroopers landing all around them. The pictures were dramatic and memorable. Nicholson walked up to the soldiers and said, 'I'm Michael Nicholson, welcome to Cyprus.' Everyone wondered how Nicholson happened to know where they were landing. He admitted that it was complete fortune. He was only in that location because his car had broken down. So even the best operators in the business can enjoy a little bit of fortune.

And talking about a lucky break. I enjoyed a quite ridiculous day when working as a trainee in general news, rather than sport, but it is an excellent example of an abrupt turn of fortune that came out of the wide blue yonder. I can never forget when the first Sunday in June 1973 turned from desperation to jubilation. Two wonderful stories dropped on to my desk like mangoes from heaven.

I was in my first job as a news trainee at BBC Radio Leeds, and I was press-ganged into the so-called "graveyard shifts", which the established journos did not want to do. Working late evening duties was exhausting as you were going home as everyone else was going to bed. Slogging away all day on a Sunday was purgatory, as you had to find material for that day's news, but more importantly items for the breakfast show on Monday. You were also missing out on a Sunday game of soccer, a roast lunch and a few pints to wash it down.

On this Sunday, there was less than nothing happening. I arrived promptly at nine and found a blank page in the news diary. I reconstituted some material and found a few pieces of dull press-release stuff for the day's bulletins but could not find any fresh or interesting stories. It was heading for lunchtime, and a frantic phone-bashing session had produced absolutely zilch. I was thinking if I do not produce something, I will not be too popular with the news editor tomorrow. I had to flesh out the midday news bulletin by including a convoluted weather forecast. In desperation and for a last throw of the dice, I started thumbing through correspondence from listeners. I found a letter from a woman on an estate complaining about a 'plague of crickets!' It sounded a little biblical. Shouldn't it have been locusts?

I got into the car and drove down to the area, thinking this would be a wasted journey, but her description of the plague of the insects was a complete understatement. It was an amazing scene. The big green insects were emerging from a huge corporation rubbish tip and invading the estate. There were clouds of them swarming all over the houses. Windows were coated with the green monsters. It was like something from a Sci-Fi movie. I interviewed some residents who were alarmed by the intrusion and very graphic about their concerns. The woman who wrote the letter produced a stream of wonderful sound bites. 'They're horrible big green things. They get into your home. They're on your clothes. They get into your bed.' Having the creepy-crawlies ending up in people's beds was a wonderful angle. (The tabloids especially liked that quote).

I returned to the office feeling very satisfied with the material. It made a great tale. The site or sight had to be seen to be believed. The next England test match was about to start in Leeds, and I could link the cricket to the crickets. Although technically or contractually, I was working for the BBC, I spent the afternoon flogging the story to the papers as well as BBC national radio programmes.

I enjoyed an afternoon biscuit and cuppa and was feeling smug. Saved by the crickets. I had a great story for the morning and a very profitable one too. At around five o'clock, I was ready to end my shift when I was told there was someone who wanted to see me in the reception. I was confronted by an elderly gentleman wearing a check, cloth cap or billy cocker as they were known in Yorkshire. The man asked me to hit him over the head! It was an unusual request. But he was deadly serious. So, I tapped him on the skull with a plastic ruler. There was a solid sound, and the ruler nearly broke.

Only days before, on the Friday, the compulsory wearing of

crash helmets for motorbike riders had become law. The gentleman had his billy cocker reconstructed with a helmet inside. It looked like a conventional cloth cap but cleverly concealed the skid lid. As a result, he had been pulled over by the police on about a dozen occasions. When stopped or apprehended, he said to the bemused copper. 'Hit me over the head with your truncheon.' They then discovered his camouflaged crash helmet.

He was a very amusing interviewee and insisted that he had worn a billy cocker all his life and was not changing now. I went back into the office and wrote and cut another story. I clocked up a few extra hours and worked late into the evening, but it was another piece of luck and another national story. Once again, I was able to sell the tale to national radio and the daily papers. It was a bit hard explaining how the two stories had been spread over the national press, but no one seemed to pursue it. I calculated on that one Sunday, I had reaped the best part of a month's earnings. A series of cheques kept plopping through the letterbox over the next few weeks. From feeling, 'I don't like Sundays', I was thinking about 'Good day Sunday'.

Another slice of fortune and a big international story also fell my way after an astounding coincidence. I was on a plane to Geneva to cover one of the UEFA Cup draws in 1999. It was not too exacting a task. But, that morning, all the national daily papers had a story plastered across their front pages about a new world record, the breaking of football's £30 million transfer barrier. Italian striker Christian Vieri had been sold by Lazio to Inter Milan for £32 million. There were plenty of pictures and profiles highlighting this extraordinary deal. At that time, Vieri was by far the most valuable player in football history. On the flight, we all read the stories and talked about the transfer.

The job in Geneva was simple enough. Often 'away trips' turn into a hard-working chore, with all sorts of gremlins cropping up, but this was a jaunt. We went to the UEFA draw and sent a report back by satellite from the shores of the lake. We then went out into the city to find somewhere to eat. The problem was that Geneva seemed to close at about ten o'clock. We found a little Italian bistro just as the owner was turning the sign round to closed. After a little persuasion, he agreed to let us in and put the closed sign back up. We were the only customers in the restaurant and sat chatting after ordering some drinks.

After another fifteen minutes had passed, the door opened, and a man wearing a blazer with an Italian badge and tie, white shirt and grey slacks wandered in. A well-built athletic guy. I produced one of those 'look twice' moments to confirm my first impression. I whispered to my colleagues, 'don't look now, but Christian Vieri has just walked in!' My cameraman looked up and in a loud voice, said, 'fucking hell, it is him!' The coincidence of the man of the moment turning up like that are probably extremely long odds.

It turned out Italy had been playing Switzerland in an international and he had popped in for a meal. Vieri had been born in Italy but spent all his early years in Australia, so he spoke perfect English. It transpired he was an avid Aussie cricket fan and was more interested in talking about the Ashes tests than football. After we had enjoyed a chat with Christian, Italy's celebrated manager Marcello Lippi joined the table, closely followed by two more of the nation's star players, Fabio Cannavaro and Christian Panucci.

We all stayed in the bistro until two a.m. The four Italians only drank a glass of mineral water and had a plain bowl of pasta each. The curious occurrence was, at the end of their spartan meal, instead of one of the extremely wealthy players settling what would have been a tiny bill, they split it into quarters. They spent a lot of time working out how much they needed to pay, and after a few earnest calculations, they each fished a few francs out of their pockets.

If you have a career as a sport reporter, keep a few mementos, especially pictures. That is something I wish I had done more. But I have a lovely picture of Muhammad Ali and I shaking hands after a TV interview, which now hangs over my fireplace. A plumber came around to do some work and saw the picture of Ali and gasped, 'Blimey!' I told him it was a picture of me, but I did not know who the other guy was. He was not as sharp as the tools in his box, as he did not get the joke!

Pride of place also goes to selfies with two of my other sporting heroes, the famous Aintree steed Red Rum, the winner of three Grand Nationals and second place in another two. Plus, the great grey Desert Orchid.

"Dessie", as he was known, was dubbed 'the nations pet' after he had won five King George the Sixth Chases on Boxing Day, a Gold Cup, Irish Grand National and many other top races. He had a quite mystic presence as a big, gleaming, white charger of seventeen hands and a stare that lasered right through your head. It was as though he was treating you with some disdain. He really had the demeanour of a big star. The little speech bubble coming out of his head probably said, 'Sod off, you're a nobody. I am a big star.'

He and "Rummy" are undoubtedly two of the biggest personalities I have met, and both performed 'on the circuit' after retirement, opening race meetings and shops and putting in personal appearances. The only shame is they could not talk. However, I would not have been surprised if Dessie had started a conversation.

Sport reporting is never easy, especially away from home.

But first, one domestic trial. When Wolves' famous Molineux stadium was being revamped, one of the stands that was closed and derelict was used for TV coverage. Whilst out of service, the facility had been taken over by a flock, or rather a swarm of pigeons; enough to populate Trafalgar Square three times over. The result was the floors were covered in a thick layer of white excrement. Sadly, I was wearing suede boots that I had to throw away afterwards.

I remember being pitch side for a very abrasive Rugby European Cup match in the South of France between Leicester Tigers and Pau. Tigers won the game, and some of the players came over to the touchline to celebrate. The problem was that they rejoiced and revelled in front of a bank of the passionate home fans, who reacted by hurling a salvo of beer cans, most of which were full. Unfortunately, I was standing in between the crowd and the players. One full can just clipped the side of my ear. I ducked away from another, which just cleared my head and was lucky to escape unhurt as some of the cans exploded around me, fizzing with beer as they hit the ground and burst like liquid grenades. If I were so disposed to throw a can of ale at someone, I would drink it first rather than waste the contents. They take their rugby very seriously in the South of France.

I commentated on a European Middleweight title fight in Bilbao between the champion, Britain's Tony Sibson and Andoni Amana of Spain. The contest took place in a bullring. The boxers changed in pens used for the animals, which had not been extensively cleaned. And that's not bullshit, or rather it was! Not exactly hygienic, and all there was for the fighters was a large bench to lie or sit on. After Sibson won the fight on points and in such a great style that the locals dubbed him 'Tony the Toreador', I went back to the hotel to wind down. Just as I was nodding off, the phone rang. It was a call from someone at BBC news HQ. They heard I was in Bilbao and wanted me to go and investigate a possible stand-off between the police, militia, and the armed Basque separatist group ETA. It was even predicted there might be some sort of street fight. I was not exactly keen to be a 'war correspondent' but ventured into the town, which was completely deserted, apart from soldiers and police. While observing events from a street corner, an armoured car came along, and I froze as two machine guns were trained on me. I pleaded the innocent abroad stuff and went back to the hotel. Fortunately, the rest of the day and night passed incident-free as the ETA group did not appear, and I was able to get back on the morning flight.

As I mention later, I have an aversion to rats. This next experience was like an episode out of Fawlty Towers. I was lucky to spend two separate weeks in Vietnam producing features and a documentary on football in the country. Colin Murphy, formerly of Derby County, Lincoln City, Notts County and Southend, had been appointed as Vietnam's manager with a mission to transform the nation of ninety million into a football power. The fanaticism for football in the country was quite extraordinary. At first light, people were playing on every available patch of land, in town squares and even in the front rooms of their houses!

On my first night, I sat in the hotel enjoying a beer when a huge black rat with a pink nose and paws emerged from under the bar and circled my chair. To me, it was a vile, gruesome-looking thing. I was petrified. He then ran back to his hiding place under the bar. Quite often during the evening, he would reappear and do a lap or two of the room and return to his lair. The next day the rat came out again, and I was shocked when two dainty women waitresses laid out its breakfast before serving me, they welcomed it like a beloved pet. This was not Basil or Roland rat. Some waiters came in and looked lovingly at the revolting rodent. They obviously did not see a rat as a dirty verminous creature, but as a cuddly pet. It just needed an appearance by actor John Cleese as Basil Fawlty, but I would rather have had an intervention by a large and ferocious moggy.

After a day in one-hundred-degree heat and total humidity, I went back to my room. I was seated on the loo when I was startled by a whirling green presence around me. It was a huge lizard. Once I got over the initial shock, he was quite harmless. Whenever I took a shower, he was on the ceiling, looking down. I felt a bit like a usurper as he seemed to be a permanent resident in the room. However, I was not keen on him sharing my toothpaste.

We did one shoot up-country and saw a stall where they had cobras pickled with liquor in jars. They were attractively set up with their mouths open and tongues stuck out. Our guide said the liquid was 'very good for men.' I decided I did not really need this potion to spice up my libido. When I asked the purveyor of the 'snake oil' where the creatures came from, he pointed to the nearby woodland where we were about to film. Every time we heard the slightest rustle in the grass, we jumped in fear, but gladly, we did not have a close encounter with a spitting cobra.

It is great to join the SAS of journalism – Sporting Active Service.

So, if you want to be a sport reporter, remember to – **smell the sweat, scent the liniment, feel the impact and taste the blood. That WOW Factor!**

A Brief History of Sport Reporting

Now we need a compact briefing about how it all started. Why and how did sport originate? This is my unexpurgated, unedited, potted, or potty history of sport.

The first indications of any sporting activities were probably around three million years ago, performed by Homo Habilis, probably the oldest human species we know about. It has been shown from archaeological evidence they did use some sort of tools, but there were no signs of football boots, cricket bats, golf clubs or synchronised-swimmers' make-up. More excavations are obviously needed. Further developments and the evolution of human strains becoming more sophisticated led to the rudiments of some sort of leisure pursuits being developed. Games were a natural and organic creation. They had not begun a Champions League, Ashes test matches or Formula One racing in a million years BC, but they did have their pastimes. After all, it must have been a bit tedious hanging around in the cave, sharpening flints, eating dinosaur burgers and occasionally daubing the walls. This is where Michelangelo got his inspiration to smear and bespatter the ceiling of the Sistine Chapel.

There are suggestions that stone-age folk enjoyed a little running, wrestling, spear throwing, archery and possibly horse riding. For instance, instead of impaling unfortunate prehistoric animals, or each other, with their flint-tipped spears, one day, someone had the idea of seeing who could hurl the weapon the furthest. Hence, javelin throwing was invented. Possibly the earliest sport event? The same notion would apply to the use of bows and arrows, so archery was born. It is quite natural to see who can run the fastest and who is the strongest in a wrestling match. They may have met at the granite and tyrannosaurus tavern for a game of darts or dominos.

As for horse racing, that may have occurred a little later in history. The earliest prehistoric 'horse' was the eighteen-foot high, thirty to forty ton, Indricotherium. In fact, it was more like a cross between a horse and a hornless rhino. The Indricotherium was the largest ever land mammal and weighed four times as much as a large elephant. That massive beast might have been hard to domesticate and would have needed tons of hay to keep it nourished. In any case, it would not have fitted into the starting stalls at Epsom or Ascot. It would have needed an aircraft hangar. Besides which, the jockeys would have needed to employ extra-long step ladders to saddle up. If it had competed at Aintree, the Indricotherium would have walked through 'Beecher's Brook', trampled down 'The Chair' and run amok through Liverpool.

The famous eighth-century British historian The Venerable Bede recalled an early form of horse racing. He claimed that horses were saddled up in the year 631.

The first daily newspaper is thought to be the Oxford Gazette (predecessor of the London Gazette) in 1665. There was little evidence of a typical back page or regular sport reports on witch-dunking, cudgel fighting or mole hunting. The Times started in 1788 and quite often contained articles on horse racing. In fact, there were regular race meetings back in 1174 at Smithfield during the reign of Henry the Second. Bearing in mind, this is the scene of the country's most famous meat market, I worry about the fate of the animals. Did they end up in a variety of medieval pies? Horse and mangelwurzel was popular at the time. There are also tales of a big race at Chester in 1512 during the reign of Henry the Eighth. The King had been an athletic chap in his youth and a keen competitor in the tilt yards (an area for jousting), but I suspect after a long spell of dedicated pie-eating, he would have had to put up a few stones overweight to be a jockey in the big race.

Charles the Second took a break from keeping up his production line of illegitimate children by displaying a new interest in racing. He was usually joined on his four-poster by numerous mistresses, operating on a shift system and his favourite spaniels. His output of offspring was estimated at more than twenty. Henry the First claimed a similar tally in the royal reproduction stakes. The problem for Charles's succession was, he did not have any kids born in wedlock. But he did find a diversion from his carnal affairs by issuing rules for racing. Charles was nicknamed 'Old Rowley' after one of the greatest racehorses of the day. Not surprisingly, 'Old Rowley' was a rampant stallion. Charles decided there should be heats for the big race, the plate at Newmarket, which he set up for the second Thursday in October, 'forever'. The saying goes that 'racing is the sport of kings and hobby of paupers.'

Racing continued to be a major sport and event when the first ever classic, the St Leger, was run at Doncaster in 1776. The winning horse was an unnamed filly, who was eventually titled, Allabaculia. The winning jockey was John Singleton, the nephew of the great jockey of the day, also called John Singleton, who was the son of… John Singleton. John Singleton, the St Leger winner had a son called John Singleton. The great Jockey John Singleton also produced a son named John Singleton. Not a lot of originality in naming offspring. It would have been very confusing if they had all been invited to a big party and issued with name tabs on their lapels.

Racing was rapidly developing into the pastime that was to become one of the country's biggest industries. The buying, selling and breeding of racehorses in the eighteenth century, was strictly for those with a few guineas stuffed in their breeches. In that regard, the sport has not really changed, but the use of syndicates has meant that those with only moderate earnings can enjoy ownership of a racehorse.

It is also conceivable, although there is little or no proof, that football started in stone age times. They may have kicked around a knot of animal fur or skins, as in medieval times, when they used a bundle of rags. It would have been loin cloths down for goalposts and on with the game. It is a recent theory, but maybe the pillars at Stonehenge were goalposts, and the lintels formed the crossbars. The nets were strung across between them. The druids may have acted as the referees and assistants. I am surprised that no one has come up with this hypothesis before. In the Champions League, it could have been Dinosaur Kiev against Stonehenge Academicals. I will bridge the gap from ancient to modern football later.

From early beginnings, it was not until the civilisations of Greece and Rome that sporting contests advanced as a major part of life. There are reports on the first Olympic Games in Athens in 776 BC. In those days, it was mainly all Greek, as Athens, Sparta, Corinth, and a few other top sides battled it out, but there were a few outsiders, especially from adjoining countries.

The start of competition was always held up by the vain Spartans. They were supposed to be titanium-tough, brick-hard, and puritanical. The Spartans even learnt brutal warfare tactics at junior school. 'Right class, put your maths books away; this afternoon we are going to be studying garrotting and leg-breaking.' They were the toughest kids on the block. The

Spartans coined the terms – 'come over here if you think you're hard enough,' and 'you're going home in a Spartan ambulance.' At the Battle of Thermopylae in 480BC, it has been stated that three hundred Spartans held up a Persian army of two million troops for a week. Modern research suggests the Persian force was between a hundred and two hundred thousand, and the Spartans were backed by several other Greek states and hundreds of unfortunate slaves thrown into the fray. Nevertheless, it was a monumental achievement.

But the hard men of the ancient world had a narcissistic trait of combing their hair in preparation for battle. They probably adjusted their coiffure before Olympic events. Imagine the hundred metres final being delayed while the Spartan competitors combed their hair or had a cut and blow-dry. Their other way of relaxing was to wrestle naked. That would surely put them at a disadvantage in any Olympic contest, as their opponents could apply some painful grabs and grips.

The games the Spartans and others took part in were a portent of things to come, with running, jumping, boxing, wrestling, discus, pankration (a mixed martial art cross between boxing and wrestling), pentathlon and equestrian competitions. The Greeks were a bit narrow-minded, as synchronised swimming, beach volleyball and skateboarding were still to come into the Olympic arena. The games were connected to the arts and celebrated with paintings and famous sculptures like 'The Discobolus' (The Discus Thrower). As you can surmise from the list of activities, the Greek Olympics did provide a sort of blueprint for track and field athletics.

A few years later, Rome set the scene for enthralled sport reporters with the biggest spectator event of all time, one that produced the wealthiest sporting star in history. The monumental event was chariot racing. Huge colosseums held as many as 300,000 people. Imagine the press box, quite literally up in the gods and the sport hacks of the day scratching out their reports on parchment, papyrus, or animal skins. Maybe even chiselled in stone? To be the main Chariot Racing reporter on the Rome Express and Star must have been one of the top jobs in the ancient world.

There were wealthy and illustrious backers for teams; fierce competition to sign star drivers, rather like a transfer system; the top performers were idolised; fans were fanatical, and riots and disturbances at the stadia were commonplace. It was a big part of Roman society. Does that sound like any modern sport?

The biggest star was one, Gaius Appuleius Diocles. Diocles was born in Portugal, started racing in Spain at eighteen years old and graduated to Italy's Serie A of charioteering. The mortality rate in the sport was tragically high. It was brutal, and only a few racers had long careers. Many did not get past their early twenties. The prospect of being run over by slashing, gnashing, chariot wheels or trampled underfoot by a team of horses was a frequent occurrence. There was little point in bringing on the physio after one of these accidents or incidents. Look at the chariot race scene in the original Ben-Hur film to get an idea of the carnage. It is still the best cinema sequence ever shot and that was without modern special effects.

Diocles competed just after 100 AD. He earned vast amounts of money. At the time of writing, golfer Tiger Woods' career earnings are estimated to be a pittance of about one and a half billion dollars. Diocle's winnings were estimated at thirty-six million sesterces, or the equivalent of fifteen billion dollars. Diocles was a sport correspondent's dream and a 'boy's own' hero. He won 1462 races and, in a sport with a high body count, retired at the age of forty-two, still more or less intact. His competitive trademark was to hang back a little and win with a last-gasp dash for the line. The Roman teams were all named after colours. Diocles started with the Whites, moved on to the Greens and ended up with fifteen years at the Reds. The sales of red togas with DIOCLES across the back must have been a merchandiser's dream. In the Reds' club shop they probably enjoyed a huge turnover in Diocles shirts.

Football, as I have surmised, is also an ancient sport. I speculated about stone age soccer. There are claims for early versions of the sport from all over the world. There is evidence of a form of the game taking place in Britain in the ninth century. The Historia Brittonum describes, 'a party of boys... playing at ball'. There are also many accounts in historical chronicles of Shrovetide Tuesday matches. Many are still re-enacted today. This is basically a mix of football, wrestling, rugby, barging, brawling, and boozing between groups of youths with a football somewhere in their midst. The idea was each team had to keep possession of the ball and manhandle it to a certain part of the town or village – their goal.

Games became more sophisticated when inflated animal bladders, usually from pigs, were used for the ball. Not a happy situation for porcine species. They were now not only slaughtered for sausages, bacon and chops but also to provide footballs. The first real establishment of a consistent game with a code was in English public schools in the nineteenth century. The Football Association formed in 1863 and the Football League in 1888. The game proved to be Britain's greatest export to the world, along with dandelion and burdock, mousetraps, custard, tiddlywinks and itching powder.

It is a strange fact that a form of sport reporting developed during the English Civil War, which dragged on between 1642 and 1651. Scribes devised what was almost 'a match report' on the latest battles between Cromwell's cronies; 'the Roundheads' and King Charles ' chaps; 'the Cavaliers'. Reports circulated on copied newsletters and crudely printed handouts. These were the precursors of daily newspapers. Accounts made the horrifying conflicts, like Edgehill and Marston Moor, sound like a violent and bloodthirsty version of 'It's a Knockout'.

Those seventeenth-century newsletters and circulars would love to have reported on one sport that was growing in popularity. By the turn of the eighteenth century, bare-knuckle prize fights, a precursor to the Queensbury rules and modern boxing, were starting to attract a big following and national coverage in various journals. There were accounts of fights going back to the seventeenth century. The exploits of two early pugilists, Jack Broughton and James Figg, in the eighteenth century, are well documented.

But the sport became a big national obsession in the nineteenth century. Rather like horse racing, bare-knuckle boxing attracted the royals and the ruffians. The extraordinary fact is that bare-knuckle fighting was illegal, but details of the secret location of a big fight were circularised. If authorities knew about it, they usually turned a blind eye. A ring was ceremonially erected early in the morning, in a remote spot. The spectators would arrive by coaches, on horseback, or on foot. Established on one side of the ring would be members of the aristocracy and even members of the royal family, laying down quite substantial bets. Opposite them would be a crowd of local lads, yelling in support of 'their man'. Gangs were often attached to the boxers.

The prize fighting circus produced some of the most famous names of the century including, Tom Cribb, Jem 'the gypsy'

Mace, James 'deaf' Burke, William Perry 'the Tipton slasher', Ben 'the Big Un' Caunt and William 'Bendigo' Thompson. Accounts of the fights were recorded in newspapers and periodicals, especially in the magazine 'Bell's Life'. The prize ring had its own terminology. They never referred to blood being spilled. It was always claret or sometimes crimson. A fighter was a milling cove, and he did not have a head. He had a cannister or attic. A punch to the mouth was a muzzle. The first-ever bare-knuckle contests had little or no rules. In Victorian times the use of elbows, knees and kicking were eventually banned.

The biggest fights of the day, equivalent to the trio of contests between Muhammad Ali and Joe Frazier, were the three bouts featuring William Thompson, alias 'Bendigo' and the 'Big Un', Ben Caunt. Both men hailed from Nottinghamshire, and it was the equivalent of the world heavyweight championship at that time. The tale of the tape was quite surprising. Big Ben, who was a blacksmith from Hucknall, was measured as reaching six foot two and variously recorded as being fourteen and a half or eighteen stone. One thing is certain, by the standards of the day, he was a big fella. Bendigo from Nottingham, by contrast, was just under five foot ten and rarely topped twelve stone. He would have been quite small for the modern Super-Middleweight category. The nickname Bendigo originated from an amalgamation of his second name Abednego and references to him being called 'bendy' owing to his elusive movement. But he was an extraordinary sportsman and was credited with inventing the southpaw stance, although he was also a switch hitter. Bendigo competed in throwing and running events, as well as cricket and many country sports. He was an awesome athlete. As a fighter he possessed wiry strength, great stamina and was lithe and elusive. Another part of his armoury was clever and often deceitful ring craft. Bendigo knew every sly trick in the book and invented a few more. At the time of his fights with Caunt, Bendigo was able to use his skills at kicking, a technique that was still legitimate in the prize ring.

The three matches between 'Bendigo' and the 'Big 'Un' are the stuff of fables. In their first match, a non-title bout in 1835, Bendigo won in a mere twenty-two rounds. Caunt was disqualified for hitting Bendigo while he was sitting in his corner. One scribe of the day wrote Caunt was, 'full of trickery and treachery.' While Thompson was, 'as deadly and as poisonous as a rattlesnake, with about the same ethics.' The fighters shared a purse of £25 for the contest, which was quite lucrative for the day.

The second contest, three years later, which was for the heavyweight title, lasted seventy-five rounds. Caunt raised his gloves after Bendigo was disqualified. Big Ben had made a few attempts to strangle his opponent in their contests and tried 'the tactic' again in the thirteenth round. In the end, it was Bendigo who was disqualified for falling to the ground without being hit. This was deemed a foul.

The third classic match, again for the title, was a lengthy ninety-three rounds! To add a caveat, many rounds were 'non-events', with the boxers idling, posing, showboating, circling the ring, joining in a bit of banter with those at ringside or locked together in wrestling holds. Bendigo also used plenty of 'verbals', constantly referring to Caunt as a 'clodhopper', he was also able to make up funny rhymes about his opponents and recited these during the fight. A further Bendigo tactic used against Caunt and other pugilists was to pull funny faces. A stunt the crowds loved. Another of his popular moves was to somersault across the ring.

It was a dirty, grudge match, with supporters of both men providing a menacing backdrop. Bendigo won the marathon despite some controversy. After he had sunk down against the ropes, his opponent Caunt started to go to his corner and sat down, but Bendigo got up and pursued him. The referee decided it was a foul, as Caunt had fallen or touched the mat with his knee without being struck. So, Bendigo and Big Ben battled it out for a total of 190 rounds without a clear outcome.

Bendigo did not fight again for five years and went back to his favourite pastime of fishing and won All-England fishing awards. He also became a preacher. Bendigo and Big Ben were rather more than prize fighters, they were two of the biggest celebrities in Victorian Britain. Bendigo had a town in Australia and a famous racehorse named after him. When he died in 1880, thousands attended his funeral procession, which packed both sides of the road as it made its way for four miles into the centre of Nottingham. Ben Caunt was the celebrity landlord of a London pub for a few years, but he died of pneumonia at the age of forty-six. There are stories that the Westminster clock Big Ben was named after him, but this may be fanciful. If only Hugh McIlvanney had been around to write some compelling articles about those Victorian scrappers!

Another big contest started in 1829 and is coming up for its bicentenary. I find it hard to believe that the event has commanded so much attention ever since. It has been turned into a big TV spectacle, a major national radio broadcast and has provided masses of copy and column inches. George the Fourth was on the throne, and the Duke of Wellington was Prime Minister when the chaps from Oxford and Cambridge decided to put down their toasted muffins and cut-glass goblets of vintage champagne to inaugurate an annual boat race on the River

Thames. It is surprising how many people grew up taking sides and deciding they were supporters of one of the famous universities. 'Are you Oxford or Cambridge?'

It is a difficult event for sport journalists to cover and gain the required knowledge and tactical appreciation, but there is now a growing band of rowing buffs. The varsity boat race has helped over the last two hundred years to stimulate the popularity of the activity, but the exploits of our rowers in recent Olympics has really expanded the coverage, both on airwaves and screens and in the increasing accounts and articles in the papers and periodicals. A lot of the credit for that goes to rowers like Sir Steve Redgrave, Matthew Pinsent, Helen Glover, Heather Stanning, Katherine Grainger and many others, whose gold medal triumphs have been celebrated by a host of new fans of the sport.

The University race has still claimed an annual splurge of national media interest, although the zeal of a few decades ago has started to fade, but in terms of attracting national interest, the race really punches above its weight. Sometimes the contest provides a great tale or two. In 1877 there was a dead heat. This caused a controversy as John Phelps, the judge who made the decision, was over seventy years old and blind in one eye. The 1912 contest provided a cracking yarn, but not for either crew. The race got underway in dreadful weather with high winds and both crews sank! Then in 1984 an embarrassing calamity. The Cambridge boat submerged before the start after running headlong into a large, moored barge. The race was rescheduled for the next day.

Yes, Oxford v Cambridge has become an entry in the Nation's diary, but it is not a race in which a host of undergraduates compete any more. It has almost become a semiprofessional contest. Some fresh-faced and young students of yesteryear have been replaced by a lot of specially imported rowing stars from around the country and the world. The teams will typically include people like Hank Wolfman from San Francisco aged twenty-nine, at six feet six and sixteen stone studying Land Economy; Bruce Billabong from Sydney aged twenty-seven, standing six feet three and weighing fifteen and a half stone and reading basket weaving and thirty-two-year-old Kaiser Van der Cheeseburger from Johannesburg at six feet eight and seventeen stone, studying sod-all. Although it has claimed a place in our sporting history, you may detect, I have become a little cynical about the varsity boat race. It is a tradition that has become a bit of a fabrication.

Like most great international sport, cricket was a British invention; although it was really a fun game that developed into a professional sport. In many countries, especially the United States, there is a feeling that cricket is contrived and overly complex, but it is a sport that's evolution was natural and innate. Nothing could be more logical or instinctive, than hitting a ball with a bat. That is the basis of many games. Cricket became popular in the eighteenth century and was played on greens and in open spaces all over the country. It was often a family pastime. Old paintings depict mum, dad and children on the village green with a curved bat, playing cricket. As the years rolled on, the game became more sophisticated, and a lot of new rules were added.

In 1709 the first ever county match was staged between Kent and Essex. Throughout much of the eighteenth and nineteenth centuries, teams played in loose groupings. It was not until 1890 that the first official county championship was held. Sport in the Victorian newspapers was now dominated by horse racing, prize fighting, football, the boat race, and cricket. In fact, cricket was starting to become big news.

In 1877 an England team, captained by James Lilywhite, set off on a three-month-long, gruelling voyage to play in the first series against Australia. Lilywhite's party were all professionals, so it did not include 'the champion' of the day WG Grace, who was an amateur. Without screens, tablets, computer games, laptops, mobiles and various music appliances, entertainment was confined to deck quoits, 'pin the tail on the donkey' and 'I Spy'. Food became a bit limited to biscuits and tins of bully-beef. First stop was in New Zealand for a few matches and then on to Australia. The players hardly had time to get used to dry land when they tottered into the first test match, which they lost. This was not surprising as they were missing their best player WG Grace (who was excluded owing to his amateur status) and their only regular wicketkeeper Ted Pooley. Pooley had been left behind in New Zealand to face assault charges.

But in the second test, England were victorious, despite coming up against Frederick Spofforth, 'the Demon Bowler'. A mean man with a mean moustache. He was to become England's nemesis for a few years to come. The tourists played around fifteen matches in Australia, but there were only those two tests, and the series ended at one-all. From that moment until the present-day, series between the two countries became cricket's most compelling competition and provided a rich vein of stories and a host of legendary and almost mythical characters like Spofforth, Bradman, Botham and WG Grace, who was later allowed to participate in the contests.

Football was also starting to gather a bigger following in Victorian society. As mentioned earlier, The Football Association was formed in 1863. The first Cup Final was held in 1872, when a crowd of around two thousand watched the Wanderers edge out the Royal Engineers 1-0 at the Kennington Oval. In the nineteenth century football had developed at public schools. The Wanderers were a club based in Upper Norwood in London and consisted mainly of former pupils of leading English public schools. Apart from winning the cup, the Wanderers only played friendlies. But over the next couple of decades, the basis of football changed dramatically as the sport became professional and nationwide. It established a bedrock in the North and Midlands. The chaps in the Wanderers were put out to grass.

In 1889 the first football league competition was concluded with Preston North End at the top of the table and Aston Villa in second spot. Other teams in the league included Wolverhampton Wanderers, Accrington Stanley and Stoke City. The game was played by toughs rather than toffs, and half-time oranges, after match Victoria sponge, Battenburg and petit fours, were replaced by strong tea and meat pies. Football was now becoming the working man's favourite activity. Britain had established the globe's number one spectacle and one of its international industries.

In 1896, the biggest sport circus was relaunched, the modern Olympic Games. As in the ancient festival, the new games were first staged in Athens. The old Olympics were organised to the glory of Zeus, the father of gods. The modern Olympics are now established in honour of Adidas, Nike, Coca-Cola, and McDonalds. There are a lot of similarities between the old and new games. As I highlighted earlier, ancient competitors came from City States and other countries. The winners got a laurel wreath around their necks rather than a medal, well, it was a cheaper option, but they did attract greenfly. The events for the new games, were broadly similar. Sadly, the Hoplitodromos a 400 to 800 metre race in full armour, carrying a shield, was dropped. Great shame! Although it is rumoured that back in ancient times, the crafty Corinthians had added DRS (A Drag Reduction System) to their shields.

THUNDER GOD AGAINST SUGAR SQUAD

ZEUS VS COCA COLA

JUNE 1ST — DIRECT FROM RINGSIDE

GOD VS FIZZ

☆☆☆ **Ringside is where it's at** ☆☆☆

A lot of the basic events in athletics were broadly similar to those staged before Christ, with a few additions. We obviously know that shot putting was invented by a big porridge scoffing, kilt wearing Scotsman, who got bored with flinging tree trunks around. However, Francis Drake's crew on the Golden Hind staked a claim by playing a macho game of boules by hurling cannonballs along the deck.

Then there was the hammer throw. That almost certainly came from prisoners in balls and chains trying to break free or enjoying a little light exercise. Another theory is that the discipline developed from the use of a delightful type of medieval weapon variously called a morning star or flail. This was a spiked iron ball at the end of a chain or pole. The idea was to whirl this around and embed it in someone's head.

As for the triple jump, in 1461 a group of Morris Dancers in the village of Blandford under the Ouse got a little inebriated after a mead drinking festival and extended their routine. The result was a hop, skip and jump.

Modern competitors do not need jingling bells or to wear that old English version of lederhosen.

The pole vault was the result of an accident in late Victorian times. A man rushed outside with the prop for the washing line on a freezing winter's day and slid on a piece of ice. He was propelled into the coal bunker and catapulted high into the air over the garden shed.

Those games in 1896 attracted fourteen nations. After that, it was onwards and upwards with more nations, competitors, venues, events, spectators, and money. The father and innovator of the modern Olympics was Frenchman, Baron de Coubertin or, to give his full title, Charles Pierre de Fredy Baron de Coubertin. As you may have gathered, he came from an aristocratic background. He famously stated, 'the important thing is not to win, but to take part.' Competitors in everything from Premiership football to village cricket or pub skittles pretend this is the case when they lose, but most sport contestants really feel it is a load of tosh.

Can you imagine saying, 'oh well, we lost six-nil, but that is not important; I just enjoyed taking part in a lovely game?' More likely, 'sod the taking part rubbish, I just wanna win.' Do you think that Novak Djokovic on losing in a grand slam final, Tiger Woods on being pipped to a major victory or Lionel Messi losing in a European final would say, 'come on now, chaps, it doesn't matter to me who wins, I just love taking part in a jolly good match?'

De Coubertin did propose the Olympic motto *'faster, higher, stronger'*, which was thought up by one of his cronies. But the Baron opposed, unsuccessfully, women's participation in the games up until his death in 1937. He reasoned that an Olympiad with females would be 'impractical, uninteresting, unaesthetic and improper.' An extraordinary selection of words and a crass irrational statement. Probably one of the most unenlightened, illiberal, and nonsensical comments in sporting history, but I suppose we can be grateful the bigoted misogynist did at least restart the Olympics.

Every four years, the Olympics provide a showcase of fabulous stories. There are just too many to pick out. For journalists, there is a stream of sporting sagas. Take your pick over the years. There was the incredible Ethiopian marathon runner Abebe Bikila. He won the gold medal in Rome in 1960. It is gruelling enough to win any marathon, but Bikila ran barefoot and set a world record. He tried some running shoes but decided they did not fit very well and gave him blisters. At the finish, he looked to have enough energy to run the course again. To prove it, he started carrying out a series of exercises like touching his toes and running on the spot. Four years later, in Tokyo, he repeated the feat of gold medal and world record, but this time wearing shoes.

Perhaps the most amazing single effort was the gold medal winning long jump by American Bob Beamon in the 1968 Olympics in Mexico City. With his first attempt, Beamon sailed through the air and nearly soared over the end of the sandpit. The jump beat the world record by an almost supernatural, twenty-one and three-quarters of an inch. His winning mark was twenty-nine feet, two and a half inches. This extraordinary jump is still the Olympic record.

There was also the remarkable tale of British race walker Don Thompson. At just five foot six and barely over eight and a half stone, Thompson was known as 'mighty mouse'. He was due to compete in the fifty-kilometre walk in the Rome games in 1960, an event that has gone into extinction. He realised that the heat and humidity would be almost unbearable during the event, but he could not afford to stop working and decamp to somewhere hot for special preparations. So, he improvised. Thompson converted his parent's tiny bathroom into a high-temperature steam room. In his first trials, he used a paraffin-heater in the room, but found he was choking on the toxic fumes. He then put on a small electric wall heater and filled the room with steaming saucepans and kettles. Thompson would then don a tracksuit and an anorak and try some sort of training and marching on the spot in the confined space. The temperature in the bathroom reached forty-nine degrees. He went through this process three or four times a week. The training routine obviously worked as he strode home for gold, fully seventeen seconds ahead of the silver medallist.

Bikila, Beamon and Thompson produced three fabulous Olympic tales. But my three favourite stories have been provided by three astonishing female athletes and three astonishing performances.

The star turn of the 1948 Olympics in London was the Dutch woman Fanny Blankers-Koen. As a child, she had been a protegee who excelled at many sports. At the time of the games, she was a thirty-year-old mother of two and was called 'the flying housewife' or 'the flying dutchmam'. She was dismissed as being too old to compete and in tune with the mores of the day, was criticised for neglecting duties at home by competing in London. The stiff-lipped critics said she should have been looking after her kids. Blankers-Koen went on to take the gold medal in the hundred metres, two hundred metres, eighty metres hurdles and sprint relay. Although, at one time, before the two hundred metres semi-finals, she broke down with homesickness, but her husband Jan persuaded her to carry on. She is the only female athlete to win four golds at a single Olympics. It was later divulged that during the London event, she was three months pregnant with her third child! During her career, Blankers-Koen set or tied twelve world records.

My next heroine is 'the Tennessee Tornado'. During a sickly childhood, Wilma Rudolph contracted double-pneumonia and scarlet fever. She also suffered infantile paralysis caused by polio when she was five. As a result, she was disabled with a badly twisted leg and had to wear a brace from the age of six to nine. But by sheer determination, she managed to play basketball at twelve years of age. At sixteen, she had developed into a top athlete and was chosen for the USA sprint team in the Olympics and won bronze in the sprint relay. Four years later, at the Rome games, the twenty-year-old Rudolph won one hundred, two hundred metres and sprint relay gold. Wilma was acclaimed as THE star of the Olympics and the fastest woman in history.

Improved technology meant the Rome games were the first to attract worldwide TV coverage, which helped to make her an international star. She was even commemorated on American postage stamps, and her story has been told in a TV movie and documentary.

After the 1960 Olympics, Rudolph took part in a big meeting at the White City when she competed for the United States against Great Britain and the Commonwealth. It was one of the most memorable events I have ever seen, with many gold medallists taking part. Rudolph stole the show with a victory in the hundred metres. She simply seemed to flow down the track with an effortless, elegant style, leaving the other competitors in her wake. Two years after her great triumph, at the age of only twenty-two, Wilma Rudolph retired from athletics. What would she have achieved with another ten years in the sport?

My third great female Olympian is, in my opinion, Britain's greatest athlete of all time. We have excelled in the technically demanding, muscle straining and exhausting multi-event decathlons and heptathlons. Daley Thompson and Denise Lewis were extraordinary. Katarina Johnson-Thompson is continuing the trend and tradition. But for me, the greatest of them all is Jessica Ennis-Hill, especially after her incredible gold medal showing at the 2012 London Olympics. The extraordinary fact about Ennis-Hill is that she is only about five foot five inches tall and a little over nine stone. She was up against many competitors well over six foot and ten stone, a great advantage in throwing events and the high jump. Ennis-Hill also suffered more than her fair share of injuries in her career, once being side-lined for a whole year. She made a remarkable start to the Olympic Heptathlon, scorching home in her hundred metres hurdles heat in an amazing 12.54 seconds. Her technique, skill and strength are simply awesome. She ended her time in athletics after taking eight major championships, including three world golds.

It is great to celebrate and recall wonderful triumphs and achievements in events like those celebrated by Blankers-Koen, Rudolph, and Ennis-Hill. It is a myth that sport journalists are doom-mongers. I remember one top football manager, on the first morning after his appointment, attended a press conference and announced in a surly manner, 'here come the vultures.' Nothing like establishing cordial relations with the press straight away. Perhaps he did not appreciate that it is always better to be reporting on success and victories than failure and defeats. Who wants to turn up to do interviews at a newly relegated football club, with a boxer who has just lost his world title or any competitor who has just suffered a humiliating defeat? It is torture and torment for everyone and uncomfortable for the interviewee.

But in the Olympics, the debacle of the London Games in 1908 produced a string of barely believable, farcical stories for the press to feast on. It was like, 'Carry on at the Olympics'. Or 'Chariots of Dire'. A complete farce.

You could not make it up!

To be fair, Italy had pulled out of the games, deciding the costs were too high. Apparently, an eruption of Mount Vesuvius in 1906 put the Italians behind in their plans; so Britain stepped in. The organiser, Lord Desborough, a fine sporting gent, was given permission by King Edward the seventh to stage the games. Desborough was not an inactive aristocrat but the complete opposite. He had rowed for Oxford and scaled the Matterhorn. More than four thousand labourers sweated and strove to get the stadium ready. Health and safety were not so closely observed in the early days of the twentieth century, as a result there were hundreds of accidents and some fatalities.

The organisers ran short of money, and the games were paid for by gifts from Lord Desborough's generous chums. A sum of eighty thousand pounds was also raised from a public appeal. Gifts and handouts were all very well, but what was needed was a shed load of hard cash, more preparation and better organisation.

So, the 1908 London Olympics got underway with a catalogue of comical and calamitous incidents. Athletes from all over the world turned up for events that were not staged or were cancelled.

A part of the protocol was performed in the march past of competitors. They were requested to dip their national flags to King Edward the Seventh and his family who were sitting in the main stand. It appears that the games' organisers committed a bit of a boo-boo by forgetting to include the United States flag amongst those fluttering over the stadium. The Americans were outraged. So, their flag bearer, not a man to argue with, a six-foot-six and nearly twenty stone shot putter called Ralph Rose, refused to dip his standard to Edward the Seventh. The King was miffed by this lack of etiquette from an old colonial and turned tail to head back to the palace. He threw his toys out of the carriage and immersed himself in a large gin and tonic. Edward took umbrage and did not return to the stadium.

Chaos and fiasco characterised the rest of the games. Events like the javelin, running, football and cycling went on at the same time in the huge, seven hundred feet, long, White City Stadium. It must have been a little unnerving for runners and footballers trying to play and compete with javelins flying around. More by good luck than judgement, no one was speared or skewered to the track.

It was all a question of 'make do and mend', with a lack of finance and far from ideal preparations for such a prestigious event. Swimming events were held up, as the water in the pool had not been changed. It was reported as being very smelly and dirty. Top Olympic swimmers did not really want to plough through a soup of toenails, band aids and body fluids. In some events, the water was so murky competitors were colliding with each other.

One of the most comical stories happened in the blue riband four hundred metres race on the track. In the final, Wyndham Halswelle of Britain faced three Americans. One of the trio, John Carpenter, was disqualified for impeding Halswelle. This was quite controversial. In the United States, the rules of athletics decreed runners could deploy a bit of blocking and barging. In the British version of the regulations, this was not allowed, and disqualification would follow. Can you imagine shoulder charging and body checking in a marathon that would add to the entertainment and severely cut down on the number of finishers?

A riot followed among the spectators. The officials held a meeting and decided the race was to be re-run the following Saturday. The Americans refused to take part, and Halswelle was told to run the distance on his own to take the gold. Why he bothered to run at all is surprising. He could have strolled around for victory dressed in top hat and tails, with a cigar and glass of champagne. Halswelle is the only person in Olympic history to win with a walkover.

One big triumph for Britain was by the City of London Police. Their powerful team won the gold in the tug of war. This was also clouded with controversy. GB swept the board in the event with three different police teams first, second and third. The Gold went to an outfit from the City of London Police, the Liverpool constabulary were the runners up, and a team from the Metropolitan Police took the bronze. The Americans objected to the advantage the British coppers gained from their footwear. The New York Evening World writer might have been tainted by a few sour grapes. 'What was our surprise to find the English team wearing shoes as big as the North River ferry boats, with steel topped heels and steel cleats in front of the soles, while spikes an inch long stuck out of the soles.' What did they expect the British teams to wear, carpet slippers? The Liverpool team threw down the gauntlet, saying they would take on all-comers in bare feet. The Americans did not take up the challenge. At the very least, after the saga of the missing Stars and Stripes, the Wyndham Halswelle barging episode, and the tiff over the tug of war, the UK and the US have developed that "special relationship".

An extraordinary fact about the games was they lasted over six months. It was 187 days, to be precise. The overall result of the Olympics was that Great Britain topped the table with 146 medals, and the USA was second with 47 medals. A great way to put Americans in their place, 'hey buddy, look what we did to you in the 1908 Olympics.'

The Scots have always produced plenty of great innovators. Robert the Bruce masterminded Arachnology. William Wallace, or was it Mel Gibson introduced face paints, although both Boudicca and Alice Cooper have laid claim to its origination. Less notable Scottish creations include James Watt's steam engine, Alexander Fleming's discovery of Penicillin and John Logie Baird with the television; but one of Scotland's greatest ever inventions is golf. Another major British export to the world.

It is not clear how golf was invented, but many nations have originated similar games in ancient times, but there is no doubt the modern game of golf was developed in Scotland. It is thought that the idea was sparked when a picnicker dropped a hardboiled egg, and it rolled down a rabbit hole. There are references to golf being played north of the border in the fifteenth century, and the legendary old course at St Andrews was first marked out in 1764. The inaugural Open Championship was first played for as long ago as 1860, won by Willie Park Senior. It was the first of his four wins, but 'The Open' had become a family affair as Park's brother Mungo won the title, as well as his son Willie Junior.

The achievements of the Parks were somewhat overshadowed by the magnificent Morris men. That is old Tom Morris and his son, young Tom Morris. Old Tom won four of the first eight Open Championships and became both the greenkeeper and professional at St Andrews. His son Young Tom Morris, or should it have been 'Morris Minor', won four consecutive Opens before the age of twenty-one. His first was at the age of seventeen in 1868. The Morris men were dedicated to St Andrews. Sadly, young Tom passed away at the age of twenty-four. Old Tom outlived his son by quite a distance, dying at eight-six. They were both born and died in the small Scottish east coast town, which has become the world's most celebrated golf centre.

Origins of Rugby are fascinating and have produced quite a turnabout in the two codes that developed. The story goes that the fellows at Rugby School were playing a game of football in 1823, when a bounder of a lad called William Webb Ellis picked up the ball and started to run with it in his hands. His pals all yelled out, 'I say old boy, you can't do that. It's not cricket.' Webb Ellis may have repented at some time as he went on to be a vicar.

A while later, after the game, the schoolmates sat down and had a collective brainstorm in the dorm while gorging on hot crumpets and raspberry cordial. Fotheringay senior, Aubrey-Smyth minor and Campbell-Bannerman scratched their heads together, producing a cloud of scurf. After some deep thought, Fotheringay said, 'I say chaps, we've invented a new wheeze here.' They wrote down a few rules on the back of a suet packet, and Rugby Union was born. They then got Bunter to eat a few extra lardy cakes and sit on a football for a few hours to squeeze it into an oval shape suitable for running and handling. That is the true story of the origins of rugby. Well, near enough.

It was at Cambridge a little later, the first 'football' team is believed to have been formed. A written set of rules was devised at Rugby school in 1845 and another version at Cambridge in 1848. By 1863 the tactic of hacking (kicking players in the shins) was outlawed. Someone always takes the fun away! The sport was really established when the Rugby Football Union (RFU) was formed in 1871.

The division of Rugby into two codes was one of the most famous and acrimonious splits in British Sporting history. It was just about the biggest social divide since the English Civil war kicked off in 1642. The rift was principally all about one thing…

money. The division also highlighted the economic and cultural divide between the North and South of England in Victorian times, and we are still trying to alleviate this cultural chasm with talk of creating a 'northern powerhouse'.

The quarrel was quite simple; those in the North wanted payment for playing to compensate for loss of earnings. It was a big commitment representing your city, town, or workplace, having to pay for transport and meals and not getting any expenses. Rugby was a working-class sport in the North. In the South, the game was represented in the main by middle classes, professionals and students. Meetings between the two sides of the argument were often heated and blunt.

Those wanting payments were mainly from Yorkshire, with some from Lancashire. The two parties were poles apart. The conversations went something like this…

Colonel Algernon Chalfont-St Giles, quaffing dry sherry and smoking a Havana cigar, representing the South. 'It's all about playing the game, old boy. It's about the camaraderie, wearing the badge on the blazer and getting together over a glass or two and some sandwiches afterwards, not about something as vulgar as money changing hands.'

Nathaniel Sowerbutts, guzzling brown ale and enjoying a pipeful of old shag, representing the North. 'Nay lad, yer talking tripe. Our lads need brass. If they play the game and have time off, they need some bloody compensation. They're from Huddersfield and Halifax, not Harrow and Hampstead. They work in the mine and the mill, not the ruddy stock exchange.'

The parting of the ways happened in 1895, when twenty-two clubs in the North broke away from the Rugby Football Union. They formed the Northern Rugby Football Union, which eventually became the Rugby League. The decision was made by the clubs at a meeting in the George Hotel in Huddersfield. In 1906 major alterations were made to the code, with the change to a thirteen-a-side game and the introduction of a simple 'play the ball' instead of rucks and mauls. Rugby League has now passed its 125th anniversary.

Affairs have gone full circle. With the Rugby League paying cash, many Rugby Union players swapped codes to earn some dosh. Two great Welsh outside halves, David Watkins and Jonathan Davies, forsook the amateur game to benefit from the professional ranks. Top England prop forward Mike Coulman was also a convert to League. But after the establishment of Union as a professional organisation in 1995, many notable changes of code went in the other direction. England benefited from the performances of former League stars, Jason Robinson, Chris Ashton, and Andy Farrell. New Zealander Sonny Bill

Williams switched codes so many times I have lost count.

Rugby Union had always been run by 'the blazer brigade', but with the onset of a professional organisation, new administrators realised the commercial opportunities. The first professional season was 1996-7, and it was a bit of a shock for some of the more conservative-minded traditional clubs. Several were bought up by businessmen and entrepreneurs. Many clubs did not have big enough stadia for the game and managed to share facilities with a local football team. In the next chapter, the economic boom for Rugby Union is highlighted.

Players moving between the two codes now are becoming a rare breed. The reason is owing to the development of new laws in both games. League and Union are both different from the versions of twenty or thirty years ago and becoming two completely different entities. It is a challenge for a league star to find a position he is accustomed to in union and vice-versa. For example, the job of a hooker or scrum half in Rugby League is vastly different to the role in Union.

This was brought home by the move of League star Sam Burgess to Union, an eighteen-stone prop forward in League, converted to an inside centre in Union. A positional change that is hard to comprehend. It is a testament to 'Slamming Sam's' skills that he could make this extraordinary transformation. Not many Union props could feature as a centre, although Burgess' transition was not a complete success in the 2015 World Cup.

Tennis is another sport with an interesting historical background. The first evidence of a similar activity to the modern-day contest was in France in the twelfth century. This though was an activity where contestants hit the ball with the palms of their hands. Before about 1850, the only game referred to was real tennis. This was a format that was established indoors in galleries in palaces. In the sixteenth century, rackets replaced palms to propel the ball. Henry the Eighth was a big fan of the game, along with jousting, riding, gorging, draining vats of booze and collecting and disposing of a series of wives.

Lawn tennis developed around croquet and bowls in the nineteenth century, and Birmingham was the epicentre of the game's development. That is not surprising in a city that invented the bicycle bell, windscreen wipers, postage stamps, electric kettles, x-rays and pacemakers; but the turning point in the sport was another British invention from the Midlands that virtually made the game possible. A machine that has become a 'keep up with the Jones' status symbol on some suburban estates – the common or garden lawnmower. Have you got a 'sit on' model? The mower was the brainchild of Edward Beard Budding from Gloucestershire in 1830. With this wonderful grass cutter, lawns could be shaved right down for the game of tennis to create a flat surface and true bounce. During the last half of the century, the sport picked up a following very quickly.

Lawn tennis was devised by a 'major wally', in fact, Major Walter Clopton Wingfield, in the early 1870s. He developed it as an outdoor form of real tennis. The first Wimbledon final was held in 1877 with an audience of just two hundred, who paid one shilling for the pleasure. There is no record of punnets of strawberries on sale! It was the world's first lawn tennis tournament. The Gentlemen's singles competition was the sole event staged. There were only twenty-two players in the first-round draw, and each player paid a guinea to take part. The eventual winner was the estimable Spencer Gore. Gore was a gifted all-round sportsman who also played first-class cricket for Surrey. He took home twenty-five guineas in prize money. The aim of the tournament was to raise enough money to pay for repairs to the roller for the grass courts. They raised a mighty profit of ten pounds and decided that Wimbledon would become an annual event.

Another all-British invention and now a big money worldwide sport is snooker. It was devised by British army officers who were stationed in India during late Victorian times. The simpler game of billiards was popular at the time, and snooker could be played on the same table. Billiards was first established around the start of the nineteenth century and became popular in the British Colonies, which is where snooker began as an offshoot of the original game on the green baize. Officers in the mess were getting a little bored by being fanned by the punkawallah, refreshed by the teawallah, and fed by the toasted-sandwichwallah. So, they took off their pith helmets and, after a lot of debate, deliberation, and drunkenness, came up with a new game. It was titled snooker after an old military term for rookies.

At first, it was a game for the gentry. Clubs with a snooker table would not let the riff-raff in. It was a case of a large pink gin or whisky and soda to be swilled while enjoying a frame or two and discussing the latest manoeuvres in Bengal and Bangalore. Snooker was strictly for the officers. Steve Davis, Jimmy White, and Ronnie O'Sullivan would not have got a game. Luckily, the tables were turned, quite literally, and ended up in dedicated snooker establishments, bars and working men's clubs.

The start of motor sport was probably a car race between Paris and Rouen and back again in 1894. Since that time, all sorts of competitions have been created on and off tracks. The blue riband event for motor sport being the Formula One series. There are several contenders to be the first Formula One Grand Prix and plenty of debate and argument, but once again, we can claim a

British triumph. The first under the rules of the FIA (Federation Internationale d'Automobile) was in 1950 at the converted wartime airfield at Silverstone. This was titled the FIA World Championship of drivers. The event was given an official sanction by the appearance of King George the Sixth. Sadly, there was not to be an English winner for this inaugural race. Giuseppe Farina of Italy took the chequered flag in an Alfa Romeo.

But all sorts of vehicles or adapted contraptions have been raced. These include trains, karts, trucks, school buses, garden sheds, snowmobiles, swamp buggies, lawnmowers, rickshaws, Reliant Robins, bathtubs, shopping trolleys, caravans and many more.

There are too many British sporting inventions to mention, but Hockey was another, although its ancestry could be claimed by Egypt, Ireland, or Inner Mongolia. Did the Mongol hoard of Genghis Khan take a break from their conquests to play hockey? With those clubs, they could have turned it into a very physical head-splitting contest. Maybe on horseback, whirling the sticks round their heads, like an all-in polo match. What we can chronicle is the game was played in schools in the eighteenth century. By the nineteenth century it was firmly established. The first club was inaugurated at Blackheath in 1849. Now all-weather pitches have increased the sport's popularity for players and spectators. They have also elevated the sport into a compelling Olympic competition.

When people ask, 'what did the British do for the world?'... *A Roll of drums and fanfare of the National Anthem. Rule Britannia. Britain is best.* The answer is simple; we devised almost every major sport. Football is the global game, rugby and cricket are being played in more and more countries. We launched tennis and golf and countless other activities.

It must be admitted that we did not create synchronised swimming, arm wrestling or camel racing – the Ascot stewards rejected the prospect of the latter activity. But we did lay claim to the Eton Wall Game, Knurr and Spell, Caber Tossing, Lawnmower Racing, Snail Racing, Tin Bath Racing, Welly-Wanging, Black Pudding Hurling and Dorset Knob Throwing. An endless list of great British sports. I rest my case!

It is also important to bear in mind the Brits invented motorised roller skates, amphibious caravans, flying bicycles, the snogometer, musical frying pans, anti-garrotting cravat, moustache protector, ventilated hat and the toothpaste squeezer. So, we have not just excelled in sport. There is an awful lot to be proud of.

Economics and Sport

Economics was dubbed the "dismal science" by Scottish writer and historian Thomas Carlyle, but it could also be called the dreary or bloody dull science. Sadly, it cannot be ignored. The days of amateur activities and the Victorian ideal of the Corinthian athlete are long gone. All sport is now in the grip of economics and subject to the machinations of high finance. Huge investments are needed for most games to function effectively. Sport is now governed by budgets, wages, transfer fees, contracts, sponsorship, and balance sheets. Sport is a business, but in some ways, it always has been, despite the rapid increase in money involved in our favourite games. I never volunteered to cover stories about sport organisation's balance sheets, clubs going into receivership or the signing of big commercial deals. I preferred action on the field; but action off it is becoming even bigger news!

Football has been wrongly described as a 'licence to print money'. Most clubs run at a loss, often many millions. Sound business practices often go out of the window when wealthy owners consider the prestige and position of their club. They want the football team as a form of status symbol and would like to glory in its success. It is a gamble. The economic theory goes like this; if we invest more and go further into debt, can our spending trigger a boom by being successful on the pitch and winning lucrative trophies and competitions? Or will we sink further into the red and claw our way out by selling precious assets, like our top players? The best comparison – it is a bit like the government. Despite protestations, they often do not know what they are doing and nor do many football clubs. Shall we raise the price of season tickets or sell our top striker for a big fee? Is it time for an increase in income tax or a cut in corporation tax? Who knows? Let us try it out and see if it works.

At the centre of the soccer money-go-round is the transfer system. Perhaps surprisingly, the first big football transfer was conducted in the North-East, between Middlesbrough and Sunderland in 1905. The striker Alf Common was sold for one thousand pounds. A whole grand! He left Sunderland for Middlesbrough, where he scored fifty-eight goals in a hundred and sixty-eight appearances. Common would have been a giant in any generation. He was six foot eight inches tall. It is extraordinary that the fee was very roughly equivalent to only half a million pounds today. Amid national outrage, the move was described as immoral, parliament added, 'where will it ever end?' It was only just beginning!

In 1928, the fee for Commons was eclipsed when Arsenal paid Bolton ten thousand pounds for David Jack. Or to give his full name David Bone Nightingale Jack. In those days, Jack was termed an 'inside forward'. The tale of the transfer has become a classic in 'how to conduct a business transaction'.

The carefully calculated plot was allegedly the brainchild of the legendary Arsenal boss Herbert Chapman. It made for a classic one-act play. He invited the Bolton delegation down to London for talks. In the bar, the Arsenal representatives pretended to be drinking gin and tonics and whisky and sodas, but the barman was instructed to serve plain tonic and soda to the London contingent. The unsuspecting Bolton party were plied with double whiskies and gins. A skilful subterfuge. They wanted £13,000 for Jack, but they mellowed and became compliant after several tranquillising rounds. The sober Arsenal representation now found it much easier to haggle over the price, and the slightly sloshed Bolton board happily agreed on an exact figure of £10,890. Some had thought Jack, at twenty-nine, was too old to command that sort of fee, but he played a hundred and eighty-one games for Arsenal and scored a hundred and thirteen goals. In his career with Plymouth, Bolton and Arsenal, he scored at more than a goal every two games, two hundred and sixty-seven in five hundred and twelve matches. Jack is one of only three players to score a hundred goals in the top-flight for two separate clubs, along with Jimmy Greaves and Alan Shearer.

By 1979 a football transfer hit the million-mark... well, nearly. Trevor Francis moved from Birmingham to Nottingham Forest for a reported seven figure fee. The real amount was £975,000. The idea of being a few quid short was to save Francis from the stigma of being the first million-pound man. Ever since, the football transfer graph has soared steeply upwards. We are heading for a £200 million pound plus valuation. It is only a question of when and who.

The engine of the football economy is basically oiled by money, cash, loot, readies, large cheques, used notes, brown paper envelopes, expensive gifts, inducements, and offshore accounts. To be fair, football is attempting to clean up its financial act as the authorities are trying to crack down on any monetary malpractice in the game.

Transfer activity is at the centre of football. It is, in many ways, the lifeblood of the sport, as well as providing a lot of drama. Small clubs make enough cash to keep afloat if they sell a promising player for a big price or enjoy a lucrative run in one of the cup competitions. While big clubs pay for a top star to fund their quest for championships and trophies. So sound investments in playing stock make that soccer money-go-round. As I stressed, it's either big spending in a plan to win remunerative big prizes or shrewd buying and selling to keep the wolf from the door.

Transfers are not as simple as the days when Arsenal signed David Jack for a mere £10,000 plus, over a round or two of gin and tonics and tonics without gin. One cheque was written to complete the deal, with only three or four people present.

Modern transactions to sign world-class players are incredibly complex and involve labyrinthine negotiations with a bigger and bigger cast. The thrashing out of a multi-million move can take an inordinate amount of time, especially when it involves a player moving countries. In this instance, they are usually represented by several interested parties. There are players 'owned' by several agents or a syndicate. So, I present. A one-act play, with just a tiny bit of exaggeration, on a typical piece of Premiership transfer business.

'THE BIG DEAL'

It is the chance for Britain's richest club, the multi-billion, Finchley Forest East (FFE), to clinch the signature of a Brazilian world cup superstar, Alberto Vasco da Gama Costa-Lotta (known as 'Jim'). The player turns up an hour late to open talks and brings his 'negotiating team' with him. On his side, crammed around the boardroom table are his agent, business advisor, lawyer, accountant, personal assistant, interpreter, sponsor, hairdresser, personal trainer, spiritual guru, manicurist, colonic irrigationist, model girlfriend Vivienne Voluptura, father, two brothers, Uncle Pedro, French bulldog and a few hangers-on. The talks are scheduled to last weeks or possibly months, with reams and reams of small print on a contract as thick as a lorry driver's sandwich.

T

Bernie Cromwell-Cash, the tycoon who has made his millions from making missile launchers from recycled yoghurt and pot noodle containers, the Chairman of FFE, addresses the multitude. He is accompanied by the club secretary and several directors.

'We're looking to pay out a price of whatever it takes, give or take a few notes, and would be willing to agree to separate deals on a few other issues, including a percentage for a sell-on fee. The player certainly wants to join FFE.'

Salazar Sleazo, Jim's agent, 'Our position is very clear Senor Bernie. We would like forty-five million paid in used English bank notes to an account in Worthing, forty- five million dollars put into an account in Turkmenistan, another thirty-five million in Kruger Rands, twenty-five million worth of uncut diamonds, an original 'Banksie', five million shares in a Dutch skiing holiday development in Jim's investment portfolio. Ten million points on his Tesco Clubcard. Ooohhh yes, and a season ticket for Catford Dog track.'

Bernie Cromwell-Cash, 'I could just write out a cheque from the Eastbourne and South Shires Cooperative Building Society. If it's all the same to you.'

Fabrizio Fabifundo Jim's Accountant, 'No, no. No Cheques. That is far too complicated. Our system is much easier. I make sure this deal is straightforward for everyone – and also for Jim as well. What do you think, Jim?'

Jim, 'Sim, Sim.'

Barbarella Buzzardo, Jim's Personal Assistant, 'Before we look at anything else, we have to come up with suitable accommodation. We will need a lot of bedrooms for Jim and his team. And an Olympic-sized swimming pool. We will also need a cinema room, a well-equipped gym and a bar.'

Jim, 'Sim, Sim.'

Mahatma Moses-Manson, Jim's Spiritual Guru, 'We particularly like this house in Windsor, it's a big enough spread and would like to buy it quickly. Can we get it sorted?'

A picture of the house is handed over to Bernie Cromwell-Cash.

'He can't bloody live there; that's Windsor Castle where the Queen resides.'

Salazar Sleazo, 'We know that, but we check it out; she's never there, it's empty for most of the year, so surely if we make an offer ...'

Bernie Cromwell-Cash, 'No, it's out of the question. You have some other properties you are looking at?'

Jim, 'sim, sim.'

Enrico Espresso, Jim's business advisor, 'Yes, we have two others we want if Windsor is not negotiable. There's this one called Longleat, with lots of animals, so Jim's pet Hyena will be at home, and one in the countryside called Chequers, which we would like to purchase from your British Government.'

Jim, 'sim, sim.'

Bernie Cromwell-Cash, 'I think you'll find these are not for sale unless you saw them in an estate agent's window.'

Fabrizio Fabifundo, Jim's Accountant, 'We haven't yet talked about Jim's wages. We want his £850,000 per week tax-free. We do not want to pay your exorbitant British taxes. His basic wages will be paid into an account in Azerbaijan. But we want to make it easy so that he is paid in just three currencies. All the bonus bits and pieces can then be worked out and paid *into another account.'*

Vivienne Volupturo, *'Yes, this tax is ridiculous. But we cannot just survive on Jim's basic wages. What about expenses? We need money to go shopping. Jim and I need to go to your Harrold's store, Harpie-Nichols and Preemark.'*

Jim, *'sim, sim.'*

Barbarella Buzzardo, *'I have to secure a big British deal in Jim's new underwear range. We have launched 'Jim Wear' in most European countries. They are the world's fastest-selling underpants. The new 'Cosy-Cojones Range' comes out next week. We need to get the transfer deal through so we can launch the range from what you say... Land's End to Johnny Goats.'*

Salazar Sleazo, *'We need a few add-ons to the fee. Another ten million after fifty performances, ten million after thirty goals, £10 every time he touches the ball, another ten million pounds loyalty bonus.'*

Alberto Advocado, Jim's Lawyer. *'Plus, we need a binding written legal agreement to ensure Jim never trains in the rain. He has a very delicate chest.'*

Uncle Pedro. *'We also need a fleet of six or seven of those cars, the Lone Ranger Rover.'*

Jim, *'sim sim.'*

Five weeks later, the fourth meeting between the negotiators is getting underway.

Bernie Cromwell-Cash, *'Well, I can report that we have made some progress and can get a big reduction on a season ticket for Catford Dog Track'.*

Jim, *'okay, sim, sim, yes, yes.'*

[The End]

In the 1950s and before the war, the economics of football were not too complex. On the balance sheet, earnings came from gate money and the sale of programmes and pies. The club chairman and board were likely to be local people who had made a few bucks from factories or retail industries. They generally had fat wallets but were not mega-rich. Top Premiership clubs are now owned by international figures or conglomerates worth billions. For some, the pot is virtually bottomless, but they do not always throw away their money. The economic development of Premiership football, while not necessarily being that 'license to print money', has provided many and various revenue streams and most still sell pies on match days, thank goodness. Whatever happened to those roasted peanuts?

First and foremost is the television revenue. To give an example, in the 2018-19 season, Liverpool earned just under three hundred million euros from television and broadcasting. It is a big earner, and the fees seem to be increasing by large amounts whenever a new contract is negotiated. There are often weeks when you can see a live English footy match on the TV every day. Marvellous! This ought to be guaranteed by government legislation.

The more traditional streams of gate money and season ticket sales are still contributing plenty of cash. Season tickets have become more and more prized. Fans want to be guaranteed a seat for every game, and many of the deals have been quite favorable, when compared to buying a separate ticket for each match.

Merchandising has become a major money maker. Club shops have reported record turnovers. From merchandising and clothing, several Premiership clubs are making around £100 million a year. Even in the 1960s you could not buy a Bobby Charlton, Jimmy Greaves or Bobby Moore shirt. You can now get a custom-made top with your own name on the back or that of your favourite player. Clubs make their money by issuing a newly designed home kit and change strip every season. Supporters want the latest gear, which is usually expensive. It is tough for parents with three children who all want the latest strip. The cost runs into hundreds of pounds. Expensive for families but money-spinning for the clubs. Some sides have even taken to issuing a third kit-styling during a season. These are usually ghastly and look like something dreamed up by a blindfolded Picasso after two bottles of wine.

The take from merchandising is mounting. It is also a global business. A club like Manchester United has several stores overseas. They are also setting up three 'experience centres' in China. These will include retail shops, restaurants, and big screens to broadcast the match day experience.

Advertising is also a burgeoning business. The outlets and opportunities for advertising are always increasing. There are those irritating, constantly streaming, distracting boards at grounds, space in programmes and publications. Sponsorship now applies to the naming of stadia and even training grounds, plus those lucrative logos on shirts. It is a fact that success on the field means commercial success off the field. In football, the rich get richer. Among Liverpool's 'partners' have been a sponsor for their training gear. Other backers have included a Japanese food brand, a Canadian tech co, a US fashion label, a Danish beer outlet and a Chinese car company. Liverpool has around twenty-five backers and four major partners. Most big international companies enjoy the kudos of being associated with a top football club.

Another main fundraiser is corporate hospitality. This scheme has become successful for several sports like horse racing, cricket and rugby. At a football ground, typically, you will pay an all-in price to have lunch at a club restaurant, be entertained by a former star player and get tea and sandwiches at half time and after the game. This can be very annoying for real sport fans. People on a corporate hospitality outing are often those who do not regularly attend events, if at all. This can often be seen at big venues like Wembley, where those on one of these jaunts miss the first ten or fifteen minutes of the second half as they are still scoffing sandwiches and imbibing a drink.

Schemes for top teams to pile up cash are being innovated every season. Just after the war and in the fifties and sixties there was little commercial activity. I remember, though, one team got free steaks from a local butcher's shop, if they won, and another side were decked out with cut-price club blazers from Sidney's Tailors.

The TV deal signed for the Premiership that runs until 2022 is now worth an astonishing five billion pounds. It is the largest TV domestic deal in the world. England's Premiership has gone way past Serie A, the Bundesliga, La Liga, and the Bhutan Sunday Conference to become the richest football league. In a table of the world's wealthiest based on turnover, there are usually five English teams in the top ten. Manchester United has frequently occupied the top spot.

In 1955, the most celebrated player of the time, England's Stanley Matthews, 'the wizard of the dribble', was paid just £15 a week by his club, Blackpool. That is roughly equivalent to £700 today. His annual salary would work out at £36,400, a comfortable living. Bear in mind he was just about the highest earning footballer of the day, but he was not exactly a wealthy man. By 2020 there were several Premiership players topping £250,000 weekly. This brings us on to the subject of the changing fortunes of sport stars. I remember Billy Wright telling me that while at Wolves, he lived in lodgings and took the bus in to the ground... and he was the England Captain! For a long time, there was a salary cap for footballers of just £20 per week. In 1961, after threats of strike action, the maximum wage for footballers was abolished. It was a bit like a dam bursting. Almost immediately, Fulham made Johnny Haynes the highest paid player in Britain on a fortune of £100 a week. Contrast this with some modern players filling their boots with several million a year.

The players now have all the trappings of superstars. They do not reside in digs any more and use public transport. The three favourite cars for top footballers are top-notch Bentleys, Mercedes and Range Rovers. About ten years ago, players had a craze for driving Hummers, the civilian version of the American services four-wheel drive military truck. These were massive SUVs that were certainly not eco-friendly, guzzling gas to the tune of 12 mpg.

I remember in the late fifties and early sixties, most of the Watford players, then in the old third division South or new fourth division, did not own a car. Many of them walked to the ground or travelled by bus with their kit bags. Sammy Chung used to cycle to the stadium. Centre-back Vince McNeice did drive up in a Morris Minor, and only our star striker Cliff Holton who was signed for £9,000 after a successful career with Arsenal, owned a comparatively swish car.

It is the same story in most sports. Olympic Gold winning stars of the past competed for the glory, as there was little financial reward. Athletes who became household names after winning at the Olympic Games, like Chris Brasher in the three thousand metres steeplechase in 1956, Mary Rand who won the long jump in 1964 and Lynn 'the leap' Davies, who also earned long jump gold in '64, hardly earned a penny from the sport. Now a track and field star of this ability would pocket a fortune from backing, sponsorship and appearance money. Individuals only earned more money from sport because their event or activity became more attuned to the professional era.

Some organisations were quite slow to link up with the sport gravy train. Tennis was attracting big crowds for tournaments and many potential sponsors. It was not until 1968 that the sport became professional. The Wimbledon Championships now shell out £10 million in prize money. That is offset by the high admission charges and the fortune needed to pay for a minuscule punnet of strawberries. The mark-up must be very high indeed!

Athletics was for years a 'shamateur' event. It was supposed to be an amateur sport, but top performers were given secret bundles of cash for competing in big meetings and kit suppliers handed out incentives to athletes who used their gear.

Rugby Union also operated in a shamateur fashion before going pro in 1995. Players were often offered incentives for going to a big club, like a sponsored car or help on a mortgage. There was the allocation of what was called boot money. Allegedly players would find a wad of notes in their boots or more likely pockets. Profitable and fictitious travel expenses were handed out as well.

It is often hard to comprehend most big sports are now major industries. Horse racing is the second biggest spectator sport, behind football, in the country. Some surveys in the past have even estimated it to be Britain's second or third largest industry. Just look at the cost of a top racehorse. Potential big race winners are now being bought for over £50 million. Racing is especially important as a business for the rural community. It provides 85,000 jobs and has an expenditure of three and a half billion pounds a year. The courses attract six million racegoers annually. Interest in the sport is increasing with more owners and more horses in training. There has also been a slight increase in the number of tracks, which currently stands at sixty in Britain.

A sport like golf is also a major industry. The many new courses being developed throughout the country provide a minor economic boost for an area. The courses in Britain are also big employers as coaches, greenkeepers, ground staff, admin people and caterers are needed. Golf equipment is not cheap, and the purchasing of clubs and kit is increasing. In July 2020, the sale of golf gear in Britain topped £42 million. In the same way, other sports like tennis and bowls are rather more than pastimes. Prize money has been rocketing up for the winners of Golf's majors. The victor in The Open can cash in not far short of two million dollars. Wentworth Golf Club once had a turnover of £17.7 million.

Of course, the big money is in the betting industry. The turnover in wagers on horses in this country is hard to work out, but it is estimated to be well over four billion pounds. When mobile phone betting first came in, one leading company estimated it had taken £100 million from the service way back in 2010. The bookies turnover for the Grand National has been calculated at about £250 million. That amounts to a tidy little profit for the bookmakers. Not bad for a day's work.

The point must be underlined again and again. Sport is an industry! It has also undergone a media revolution in the twentieth and twenty-first centuries. One reason is increased leisure time, with working hours getting shorter and many on four-day weeks or part-time deals. Holiday periods over the last hundred years have become much longer. Other factors to take into consideration are, people have more disposable income to spend on sport and leisure, and there is more commercial interest.

Better transport also enables fans to attend sporting events more easily. Many are now much more spectacularly staged.

Sixty or seventy years ago, a trip, for example, for Arsenal fans going to Newcastle would have been an ordeal. By road, it would have been many uncomfortable hours in an old charabanc, coughing and spluttering on single-lane roads, with no toilet on board and stops at a wayside café for a comfort break, stewed tea, a stale cheese sandwich, or cremated meat pie. Today the journey back by coach would take the best part of five hours. All those years ago, with the match finishing at around a quarter to five, the journey would have taken seven to eight hours. That means the party would not have been back in London until midnight or the early hours. The train would have been a better option, but still arduous. Now with swish coaches speeding up motorways complete with in-built toilets, plus luxury high-speed trains accommodating excellent refreshment facilities, travel times have been reduced, and conditions have become more comfortable. Although I must add a rider, this comparatively luxurious travel is expensive.

Since those times of uncomfortable treks to away matches or venues, sport coverage has grown at an extraordinary rate. In the 1950s the only major sporting businesses were football and racing. I have listed the factors which have contributed to the sport boom in the last sixty and especially the last thirty years. Sport and the media have developed into two interdependent consuming monsters.

The analogy I would use is that they are like two big hungry grizzly bears with their paws in the honeypot. When a sport club has success, it generates more money and more publicity. So, the sport bear scoops up more honey.

With extra top events going on, the media bear has more to feast on for column inches, airtime, screen time, website, and social media coverage. It is a two-way relationship. Sport bear gorges on the media. The media bear gorges on sport. They are licking their lips at the prospect of getting their paws in the honeypot. The more sport is publicised on the media, the bigger the audience, plus a burgeoning interest in commercial spin-offs.

Who would have predicted a few years ago that viewers and listeners would be gripped by rowing, netball, curling in major games, cycling and motorbike racing? Companies have failed to transform certain sports into television spectacles. There was a lot of money spent to try and manufacture squash and bowls into the next major television happenings, but all attempts failed. For squash, a see-through 'perspex court' was designed, but it was soon transparent that the sport did not translate to television.

The amount paid to top sporting performers can be illustrated by the prize money earned by World Snooker Champions. In 1927 the great Joe Davis, the father of the modern game, was the World Champ. He won a princely £6.50 for his efforts. The average yearly earnings of the day were around £130. In 2010 Neil Robertson won £250,000 for the top title. The average annual wage of the day was £25,000. Another decade further forward and Ronnie O'Sullivan pocketed half a million for winning the 2020 World Championship. The fact that snooker could almost have been created for TV has increased its popularity. You can see everything that is going on in one locked-off camera shot in a small, confined space. Tennis has a similar appeal.

Other sports have been boosted in output and revenues by TV coverage. Not many years ago, it would have been difficult to stage the 'Tour de France' as a television spectacle; but now, with satellite links, helicopters, cameras on motor bikes and many more fixed locations, the event has become a compelling TV drama.

The media has created a revolution in sport's riches, and sport has created a revolution in media coverage. Let us take Rugby Union as an example. I mentioned earlier, those who ran Rugby up until about 1990 did not realise what a great commercial product they had to nurture and develop. That all changed with the giant lurch into professionalism. For instance, the Five and subsequently Six Nations Rugby Championship was a fabulous event to market.

A few years ago, I produced a feature on the upsurge in wealth for a big rugby club. For years, Leicester Tigers was England's leading outfit. In 1970, the team got an average crowd of around one thousand, plus a dog. If it was a local derby against Coventry, they may have reached close to three thousand, plus two dogs. Media coverage was sparce. The highlights were a column or two in the local paper and a mention or two on local radio. The club turnover I had roughly estimated at around £90,000.

The game went fully pro in 1995. Just fifteen years later, in 2010, their Welford Road ground was attracting around twenty thousand people for big games. Media interest included around twenty live matches on SKY Sports. There were reports in every daily national newspaper and intense local coverage in papers and on two radio stations. The top paid players were earning over £200,000 per annum, not huge by soccer standards, but still a good salary. The turnover was around £18.5 million, with a wage bill over £4 million. The income has meant that Leicester Tigers were able to start the construction of a super new stadium. Some leading Rugby Union internationals have now been able to earn salaries topping half a million pounds in the Rugby Premiership. French rugby has been paying the highest wages to import stars from all over the world.

Another area in which commercial interests have made an impact in sport is in the way some stars have been transformed into human sandwich boards or advertising hoardings. A modern Formula One driver or Moto GP rider is festooned with adverts. Football is becoming rather similar. It will not be long before shirts are plastered with ads and logos from a few different sponsors. It does rather spoil the appeal of wearing your club shirt to be covered with ads. I would rather revert to a retro top from a few decades ago than walk around advertising one of the numerous betting companies that have sprung up.

When sponsors' names and adverts began to appear on sport competitors' clothing, TV chiefs insisted that we had to avoid them, as this was 'unfair advertising'. At first, this was quite easy. Most stars would have something emblazoned across their chests. When we conducted a chat, it was quite simple to frame the shot above the offending company name or commercial. The advertisers then issued baseball caps with logos on the front. So, the shenanigans continued. We now took a shot of the interviewee from just below the peak of the cap to the neck. The next move was that adverts and wording were put on shirt collars. Now it was a narrow shot between the forehead and the chin so that we only showed about two-thirds of an interviewee's face to avoid any offending adverts. Eventually, the TV companies gave up the game. Victory for the sports' clothing and equipment industry! If businesses and enterprises pay out a lot of money to finance sport and keep it going, then they deserve commercial space.

Just imagine trying to avoid advertising when covering Formula One. The cars are coated with commercial logos, the drivers are splashed with adverts, and there are hoardings all around the circuits.

How to work a patch

For most aspiring rookie sport journalists, or anyone working in the media, the first job, getting a foot in the door, is the most important. That can also apply to many different occupations. It usually involves 'working a patch'. In other words, you are assigned to a city, town, or part of the country to work on a newspaper, radio station, website, or, if you are fortunate, a TV producer or TV news outlet. Most young people looking for a job apply for several posts. It is a lottery as to where you may end up. 'The patch' can be anything from a region like the North-East or North-West, a big city or a small provincial town. Maybe an area of London or even an offshore island.

You are the 'new kid in town', starting your first job at a local newspaper office or on a local radio station. The first move is to hit the floor running and try to carry out some thorough graft and research to familiarise yourself with the area. For anyone starting a new job in some part of the country you are not particularly familiar with, I have this vision of a fresh-faced youngster turning up at a deserted train platform or bus station of a distant outpost or faraway place with just a couple of suitcases, pack of sandwiches, flask and map. It is a scenario that may be familiar. This is the start of your career and a chance to get some real experience over a year or so and build up your CV. If you do not like the place, there is always the chance to move on after a while. Over the first day, you may be dreaming of finding and interviewing Lord Lucan, who has been working as a clandestine shepherd for the past few decades. You might discover the definitive 'new Messi' or find the site of an ancient alien settlement in the Tesco car park. The chances are life will be a lot more mundane.

I once worked on a radio station in a comparatively remote area of England. It was my first staff job at the BBC, and I was keen to take the first post I was offered. The place turned out to be not exactly exciting, entertaining, or enterprising. The manager ran the station like Stalag-Luft One. We used to joke about jumping over the wire, dodging the machine gun turrets and making a break for it. His most famous quote was, 'it doesn't matter if no one is listening as long as we do the right job.' All well and good, but if nobody is tuning in, we are obviously not doing the right job. The office was a bit like a cross between the civil service and a monastery. Not too joyful.

It was also not a very forthcoming area for interesting sport stories. A character who was on the radio stations' so-called 'Council' was miffed I had not covered any ploughing matches. He may have had a point, but I did not see this as a major outside broadcast or audience grabber. It has not been developed into a major network sport yet. One difficulty could be that there are not many ploughing match commentators to call on. You can just imagine on network radio. 'In a moment, the football scores of the day, but before then, let us bring you all the ploughing match results.' I suffered for a year at Radio Stalag-Luft, before escaping over the wire.

For some, that first move can turn out very well. "Journos", like anyone else, enjoy being the big fish in a little pool and do not want to move on. They stay on for a long time and build their career at a local paper or radio station. That is quite understandable and can make for a great lifestyle. There is a feeling of status in the community. You become a (or the) local celebrity.

With most papers and radio and TV stations, there is a morning editorial meeting that is the stuff of sit-coms. It comprises the editor or manager, the news editor, other hacks or producers and you, representing sport. This assembly sets the agenda for the day and is accompanied by a series of yawns and grimaces. I have sat through many. It is not quite like a board meeting at a top industrial concern or company.

Those at the early get-together are usually wiping the sleep out of their eyes, wondering why they have got odd socks on, smelling of over-applied perfume and cheap after-shave, slurping a strong coffee that is dribbling down their chin, maybe salivating over a greasy bacon butty and battling to stay awake. Some are trying to stay out of sight in a corner. Yes, the 'morning meeting' is the dynamic start to the day. Make sure you enter the summit brimming with ideas. There is nothing worse than looking at an empty pad or notebook and thinking, 'I have not got the slightest idea of a story or anything going on.'

Remember you are a journalist, someone who can find a fascinating tale at the stick insect breeder's whist night or among a group of Trappist monks at their debating society. You are an expert on anything and everything for half an hour, especially with the world wide web to call on. Before going to the editorial meeting, you will have checked as many of your story sources as possible. That may mean other papers, radio stations and magazines. Social networking is now vitally important and requires constant perusing. Then do some phone bashing, checking contacts and any tip-offs. There is also gossip floating around and busybody sport agents to pursue. The other feeling or big idea is often in the back of your mind; by that I mean any hunches? Sometimes you just have a hint of something about to happen, and that is especially true in sport.

When you start to work your 'patch', the first question is, 'what have we got here? Who holds the power?' Establish your 'workshop'. Let us invent an imaginary scenario. You become the sole sport writer on the Sewertown Sentinel. The town has a struggling league-two football team; Sewertown Sloths; a racecourse Sewertown Park, and stages Championship Rugby Union, the second tier of the game, with Sewertown Ferrets. These three sporting bodies will provide most of your bread and butter, the daily or weekly stories. Turn up to training sessions and have some good informal chats. Your mission is to get to know everyone concerned with these organisations, the manager, CEO, chairperson, captain, leading players, and competitors. These are the three biggest sports, but you can search out any individual stars who may reside in the area and check out a whole raft of other activities.

Quite often, a minor sport will produce a great tale. A friend of mine once gained a lot of coverage from a local tug of war team that won the national championship. Plenty of networking is needed. You could try the Arsenal director's trick, but I do not advise it, even if drinks can loosen a few tongues and vital information may be imparted. There is also a need to get to know other big players outside of sport who may have an influence, for instance, local MPs, council chiefs, sponsors, industrialists, the movers and shakers.

One advantage, or maybe disadvantage, of working in a small area is you get invited to every 'do' unless you are a social outcast. So, you can carry out what is called networking. You become established as a person of influence or as I mentioned, 'local celebrity'. It is a conundrum, 'should I stay or should I go'. Sometimes these can be a pain, having to make polite conversation with so-called local dignitaries and brain-numbing bores over a predictably unappetising buffet and equally unpalatable beverages. You might have sampled the menu. Cheap tongue-curling white and red plonk that tastes like fruit gums soaked in vinegar. 'This Angolan Liebfraumilch is okay, have you tried the Albanian Chateau Crapeau?' The cheap vino serves to wash down the bland canapes the diameter of a toenail with half an olive and a fleck of tuna on top. Then there are pieces of the standard rubber chicken, greasy mini sausages the size of a lozenge and a few rounds of quiche that has an unedifying soggy texture. For afters, there is the stale cheese, wilting celery, and very dry sawdust biscuits, plus the inevitable trifle, that is even soggier than the quiche. Is this familiar?

There are some occasions when the social event can be forthcoming, especially for making contacts, but have your antacid tablets ready for the aftermath. At other times it is a torturous clock-watch, and you are looking for an early escape route. The host may say, 'you must have a chat with Colonel Stoat-Morton about his over sixties croquet team.' At this instance, a mobile phone becomes a valuable weapon. You look at the screen and utter, 'oh my god, something has just come up, work I'm afraid, I have to go. Thanks for a lovely evening.' Phew!

I once worked with a "journo" who quite literally went to the pub if nothing was happening. He knew which local hostelries key local characters used as their watering hole. It might be one where the local sport cognoscenti hung out and another where local politicians frequented. His method was a source of good stories and a chance to sample some fine local brews. He usually tottered back to the office in a cloud of real ale fumes, complete with a good story and a recommendation that the cheeky polecat bitter was superb.

The toughest task for the 'new kid in town' is often getting familiar with that awful term 'multi-tasking'. It basically means that a reporter *has* to carry out a lot of additional jobs to save money. Tasks the old-fashioned hacks would have been mortified to carry out. Using social media for getting information across is now of paramount importance. A newspaper writer may also have to take a few pictures these days and even video an interview. Most TV reporters did not mind carrying tripods and pieces of kit around, but now they are trained in rudimentary camera work and picture editing. You may probably never work in Hollywood as a top cinematographer, though, but multi-tasking is a big part of a "sport journo's" duties.

You will also get to know which persons are the best interviewees and provide a story or some good copy. I worked in an office where we carefully noted which footballers were the best talkers. We utilised a whiteboard on the wall with a sophisticated and highly scientific rating system. It was like a league table of loquaciousness. Every time we conducted an interview, we assessed a player's story potential. A player getting eight or nine out of ten was a top personality and could always be very entertaining or informative. Those totalling five or six were usually interesting enough and reliable. Any players getting a mark of one or two were uncommunicative, not very forthcoming, or quite simply as thick as concrete slabs. You really wanted to avoid a 'oner' or a 'two-er' for interviews.

You must attempt to mind your P's and Q's; if you upset someone on your patch, especially early on, it could create a problem. You want to keep everyone onside. Locals can get very touchy. I remember in a football match report describing a centre half as 'a man who played as though he had a bolt through his neck.' This comparison with Frankenstein's monster did not go down too well with the lad. On my next visit to the training ground, I was informed the player 'wanted to have a word with me.' At six foot three and over fifteen stone, I was worried he wanted rather more than a word. It transpired he was quite sensitive about my comment. I apologised, and we got on very well from that moment onwards. I was glad to be conscious after our get-together.

When you work a patch, you are often dealing day to day with just one football team. The problem with that situation is quite often, you need to extract some sort of story every day. Even if it is an update about a player's groin strain. There is an upside to that, as with just one club to concentrate on, you can, as I alluded to earlier, strike up a good relationship with the manager and chairman.

At one club I covered, I remember going down on a Friday to the training ground, and the manager was excited about a striker he was signing that morning who would be eligible to play on Saturday. He had confided in me that he was pleased with the number of crosses his side were getting over but was disappointed with the goal tally and felt that this new giant centre forward would put that right. As he signed the forms and posed for photos, the new frontman certainly towered over everyone, and the fee seemed to be very reasonable.

Fast forward to Saturday evening, after the team had laboured to a goalless draw at home, after the much-vaunted new boy's debut. I went into the manager's office, and he was sat at his desk with a large scotch and his head in his hands. I asked him, 'what is the matter?' And he replied about his new striker, 'blimey, I can't believe it, he's six-foot bloody four and can't bloody head the ball!'

As the new kid, the contacts file should be as full as the local telephone directory after a few months. You will also know everyone that is anyone on the patch and ease your way into the job. Your brain will be bursting with a stockpile of stories and all the local gossip. You will be the king or queen of all you survey.

Moles, Snouts and Informants

'The Sweeney', which was first televised in the 1970s and is constantly repeated, is still, in my opinion, the best crime series. It can look a little dated and not exactly politically correct today, but it was the first realistic portrayal of police officers as being flawed and normal folk, just like you and me. The dialogue between Inspector Jack Regan (John Thaw) and Sergeant George Carter (Dennis Waterman) was brilliantly scripted and often ad-libbed. They brought great clichés and sayings to the screen like, 'you're nicked!' and 'there's been a blag guv.'

Regan and Carter were also very dependent on their moles, snouts, grasses, contacts, and informants. They were usually called snouts by Regan and his crew and informants by the top brass on the fifth floor. Just as 'the Sweeney' were only as good as their snouts and informants, journalists are often only as good as their moles and contacts. Regan got reports on prospective blags from his snouts. Sport journalists get news of prospective football transfers or sackings, plus any other big news from their moles.

Building up a list of people who can provide information from within organisations can take time, but it can be like a seam of gold for breaking stories. A journalist is only as good as his or her sources. The reporter and informant establish a trust. I have used many moles over forty years as a sport journalist. Most are still friends today, but I have kept their identities a secret. So, no names, no pack drill. In my accounts of various contacts, I have changed their names.

One of my best moles was Doris, who had that anachronistic title as 'tea lady' at a football club. She catered both for the chairman and the manager, and although she may have merged into the background, she knew everything that was going on. Nothing got past her. I remember one day she whispered in my ear, 'the manager and the chairman have been having a right set-to this morning. They were shouting at each other. It was all about the signing of that Dutch lad. The manager wants him urgently, and the chairman won't cough up the money.' I thanked her very much, and as I was interviewing both the manager and the chairman that morning, I was 'well armed'. They both seemed quite startled by my grasp of the situation and, as a result, dropped their guards a little and were very forthcoming and honest. Doris provided many little snippets, juicy gossip, some super stories and a great cuppa, from a big iron tea pot, with a bourbon or digestive.

Groundskeepers at clubs can also be a good source of info. After all, they are often milling around the players when they train and overhear all sorts. You could say they have their ears close to the ground. Another contact and friend of mine, Ron, was the groundsman at a club and was very aware of all the goings-on. He was also often in conversation with the players and staff. He told me at training one morning a lad was bragging about a multi-million move he had set up to join another club. The player in question, although talented, was regarded as an arrogant git by most of his colleagues. I followed the story up with his agent and got an exclusive. The club collected a big fee and were also heartily glad to get rid of him.

A contact of mine in a certain city was one of the best

physiotherapists in the business. So much so that players at the local football, rugby, and cricket teams, did not bother to see their club physio but made a private appointment to see my pal. His clinic would often be full of stars from the world of football, rugby, cricket, and other sports. I also used his practice, and there was nearly always a sporting star in attendance to chat with. There was a time when the squad at the football club were, to put it diplomatically, not very enamoured with their manager. They wanted to see the back of him. I got all the inside gen from the physio and some of the disgruntled players.

Another friend worked at one of the leading motor racing circuits in the country. He could see what was happening on the track from his office. Quite often, in motor sports, top teams, drivers, and riders go to a circuit for secret testing. It is often quite like cloak and dagger stuff, despite the number of monster trucks turning up, providing a bit of a 'giveaway'. It was from a tip-off from my mate I acquired another interview with Ayrton Senna. He also lined me up with an exclusive story on Jaguar's return to racing and many other interviews with stars who were indulging in a 'behind closed doors' session.

Without a doubt my two top moles have been chairmen of football boards. One club launched an internal inquiry into how a television company was getting a stream of stories and inside information. The board of directors staged an investigation but could not plug the leak. What they did not realise was our source was their own chairman. He was a great friend of mine and a chum of one of my colleagues. We used to meet up with him for lunch, and he would say. 'I did not tell you this, but we are signing that French international defender on Friday morning for a club record fee.' He was always open and honest. If you asked him a question, he gave a straight answer and liked socialising with the press. He was a 'bon viveur', excellent company, plus a great fund of stories and anecdotes.

Another club chairman also kept in close tabs with me. He even got me to act as a go-between to secure a big signing. So that was quite an easy scoop. One day I was at home when he rang up. He confided that he had a short list for their new manager and asked what I thought. I gave him my opinion on who would be the best boss, and he appointed my choice. The new manager did at least last a full season before getting the axe.

There is one person who is always a useful contact. At quite a few clubs, there is a 'general factotum' or 'dogsbody'. This is someone who carried out various tasks like cleaning the players' cars, sorting out their mail and making teas and coffees. The GF has often been around for a long time, and nobody remembers when he or she first appeared at the club. It turns out that most individuals who fulfil this role are unpaid 'hangers on' who have become part of the furniture. A succession of managers may come and go, and even chairpersons too, but the GF stays in place. Some clubs need to install revolving doors for the number of bosses they appoint and dismiss.

At one team, the GF used to break off from cleaning the players' cars to impart all sorts of information, much of it was useless gossip, but there could be some useful snippets from time to time. At another club, the manager was getting more and more irritated by the GF, who was almost spending more time with the players than him. He even tried to join in selection meetings. The boss asked to have him sacked, but he could not be formally dismissed, as he did not have any form of job or contract with the club.

Commentary and Lives

For television and radio reporters, there is nothing as much fun as live broadcasts, and that applies especially to sport. The 'lives', or outside broadcasts (OBs), get the adrenalin flowing and create some excitement. There is nothing so exhilarating as being on the end of a microphone or camera and ad-libbing a report, knowing that anything you say cannot be edited out or retracted. Carrying out pre-recorded material for reports is satisfying, but nothing matches the thrill of 'going live'. Most people perform at their best, as you *have* to produce the goods and concentrate hard.

It is usually during live commentaries that some of the most memorable mistakes are made. Boxing expert – 'Sure, there have been injuries and even some deaths in boxing, but none of them really serious.'

Murray Walker motor racing commentator – 'There's nothing wrong with the car, except that it's on fire.'

David Coleman – 'There's going to be a real ding-dong when the bell goes.'

Basketball analyst – 'He dribbles a lot, and the opposition doesn't like it. In fact, you can see it all over their faces.'

Rugby commentator – 'And he's got the ice pack on his groin there. So, it's possibly not the old shoulder injury.'

Radio football commentator – 'Julian Dicks is everywhere. It is like they've got eleven Dicks on the field.'

Radio commentator – 'If that was on target. It would have been a goal.'

Another football commentator – 'I was saying the other day how often the most vulnerable area for goalies is between their legs.'

There are always difficult and painful moments when performing live. When the great Desert Orchid died, I presented a broadcast from his old stable in Leicestershire. There was a lot of nostalgia as people mourned 'the nation's pet'. His box was now inhabited by another horse, who nuzzled up to me, and I patted him on the head during the broadcast. It was a cold winter evening, and I was wearing a shirt, thick jacket and anorak. With little seeming menace, the horse leaned across me, put its jaws around my right bicep and clamped down. I did not know that a horse could bite so hard. The pain was quite extreme. I was pleased that there was only a slight gasp in my delivery. When I stripped off my clothes, my arm was bleeding profusely and in between the teeth marks was a big blue and purple swelling.

There are a few characteristics people enjoy from commentators and live broadcasters. As I alluded to earlier on, TV viewers and radio listeners enjoy watching and hearing people who have adopted a unique style. This may not be an accident, but the result of someone who has worked hard to think things through and developed some good ideas and habits. They have probably thought about who they are broadcasting to. I always feel that great communicators sound very personal, as though they are addressing one person, perhaps a father, sister, brother, or grannie.

I have three big moans about sport reports and commentaries, the wrong use of present tense, that awful word 'quality' and commentary with lots of yells and screams but no accurate description.

When presenting a live commentary, you will obviously use the present tense, telling the story as it happens. To give an example... 'Smith passes to Jones. Jones crosses from the right. Brown heads in at the far post.' But quite often, for reports on events that have already happened, broadcasters will still use the present tense, which sounds quite odd. It should now be... 'Smith passed to Jones. Jones crossed from the right. Brown headed in at the far post.'

The other gripe is the outbreak of the 'quality syndrome'. It crept into sport broadcasts about ten to fifteen years ago. Now it has become of standard use. It is a word with a rather nebulous meaning. Quality can be used as a noun or adjective. As a noun it really means 'the standard of something as measured against other things of a similar kind'. So, the word must be qualified. Are we talking about bad quality or good quality?

When used as an adjective, quality simply means excellent. Using 'quality' does not really add much to a description. It is really utilised by lazy sport broadcasters who cannot think of another word. For example, the unimaginative commentator may say. 'Brown on the right played a quality ball down the line. Jones who has displayed a lot of quality this season, chipped the ball in from the corner of the box. Smith supplied a real quality finish.'

You could use the full spectrum of the wonderful English language.

'Brown on the right played a penetrating ball down the line. Jones who has displayed a lot of deft touches this season, chipped the ball in from the corner of the box. Smith supplied a right-foot hammer blow to finish.'

I often note the 'quality count' from some commentary teams. In one match, I turned the volume right down after the tally had reached twenty before half time. I remember asking a manager about his latest recruit. He replied earnestly, 'we've signed a "quality player".' Yeah, thanks for that; it has told me absolutely nothing. You would think that anyone playing in the Premiership would qualify to be a 'quality player', if not, what are they doing there?

For anyone suffering from 'quality syndrome', I would suggest a night in, swotting up a thesaurus or dictionary. Quality bloody quality! The only person allowed to use the word is Arsene Wenger for his delightful pronunciation of 'qualitee'.

For those who cannot think of an alternative to 'quality', here is a lengthy list of various random words and phrases: ability, excellence, brilliance, skilfulness, talent, accuracy, calibre, accomplished, high calibre, class, high class, hallmark, stature, first-rate, five star, top-notch, top drawer, top flight, high standard, high grade, worth, great distinction, prime, capability, aptitude, mastery, prowess, attributes, genius, consummate, blue riband, exceptional, superlative and polished.

There is another term that is fast becoming a standard part of 'footy speak'. It is the use of the word "top". There are often references to top players, but this has now extended a little to a 'top, top player' and 'top, top, top player'. I suppose it is a sort of grading system. A 'top' player is good. A 'top, top' player is very good. A 'top, top, top' player is excellent. I have only ever heard one reference to the four-tops apart from songs like, *'Reach Out (I'll be there)'*. That was a top, top, top, top player. In this category, you would surely have to be the greatest of all time. I have yet to hear a 'top, top, top, top, quality player'.

When I am listening to a radio commentary, I like to hear a good description of a passage of play. That is easier said than done because things can happen very rapidly. But I like to hear some sort of account as a goal is scored. Often at the height of the excitement, a commentator may utter something like.

'The ball out on the right and OOOHHHH, AAARGGHHH. ITSAGOOOAAALLLL!' That has not really told me a lot.

There are some ingredients that can be mixed into a commentary or live that can really enhance the performance. You need to make sure you are accurate in your description. Remember, you are the conduit for viewers and listeners. Try to sound a bit passionate, as though you are totally absorbed in the commentary or story. You can also add a bit of drama to accentuate the events. Plenty of wit does not go amiss. That may be wit as in amusing remarks or inventive comments or phrases. Best of all, make the broadcast memorable.

Perhaps the most unforgettable piece of commentary came at the end of one of England's greatest ever sporting triumphs, victory at Wembley in 1966 over West Germany in the World Cup Final. As Geoff Hurst scored the final goal in the 4-2 win, in the dying seconds of the game, commentator Kenneth Wolstenholme summed it up by stating,

'Some people are on the pitch. They think it's all over. (*As Geoff Hurst scored*) It is now!' The timing was perfect. Probably, the most memorable piece of sport commentary in the English language. Three short sentences that have been recited by people, even born years after the famous World Cup victory.

Legendary Scottish rugby commentator Bill McLaren was another who came up with some wonderful quotes and phrases. These included ...

'Those props are as cunning as a bag of weasels.'

'It's high enough. It's long enough. AND IT'S STRAIGHT ENOUGH!' And my favourite one, 'He's like a demented ferret up a wee drainpipe.'

The doyen of live golf Peter Alliss was another who added plenty of wit and style to his commentaries. This was his analysis of golf. 'All games are silly, but golf, if you look at it dispassionately, goes to extremes.'

As for witty remarks, James Richardson came up with a possible first prize entry when talking about the subject of Andriy Shevchenko's lack of goals after being signed by Chelsea.

'Chelsea paid a levy for the Shevy, but the Shevy went dry.'

We mentioned 'quality' as being a hackneyed word. Football commentaries can often include a load of well-worn clichés that can be reeled off; "a clinical finish"; "denied by the woodwork"; "sick as a parrot"; "they're queuing up at the far post"; "a game of two halves"; "they're on the front foot"; "end to end stuff"; "he'll be disappointed with that"; "it's like the Alamo"; "setting his stall out"; "he gave one hundred and ten per cent"; "he's got that in his locker"; "schoolboy defending"; etc. Most goal frames are now made of metal. I remember in a match the ball hitting the post with a resounding 'clang' and the commentator remarking that the striker had hit the woodwork. However, I do acknowledge that the use of woodwork is metaphorical.

There is a crucial difference between TV and Radio broadcasting, and the approach to commentary is slightly different. As the listeners cannot see the match, your remarks must paint the picture, and you need to provide plenty of vivid descriptions. To state the obvious; television viewers can see what is going on. The person at the mic adds to the story and provides further comment. Hopefully, some interesting stuff. Imagine someone watching who needs your expertise.

I have heard many radio broadcasters who seem to be in fear of any silence and keep talking without taking a breath. The secret of sterling performers is the ability to pause. That will often magnify and underline an interesting or witty remark. Full stops and commas are particularly important in live commentaries. You need a pause to breathe.

Just try this first passage of commentary without any of those little punctuation marks. This could be a party game after a few drinks.

'The ball is with Smith on the halfway-line and he slips it out to Jones on the left touchline he in turn plays it down the middle where Green gets a flick on into the penalty box and White rounds Brown and lashes the ball like a missile into the top corner as Melchester take an early lead with a great goal.'

You may need oxygen after a while if you continue in that vein. Now with those little full stops and commas.

'The ball is with Smith on the halfway line. He slips it out to Jones on the left touchline. He in turn plays it down the middle. Green gets a flick on into the penalty box. White rounds Brown. He lashes the ball like a missile into the top corner. Melchester take an early lead. It's a great goal!' It is much easier when you have space to breathe.

The great TV cricket commentator Richie Benaud said, 'The key thing was to learn the value of economy with words and to never insult the viewer by telling them what they can already see.' Commentaries are usually double acts. The main voice is expected to tell the story and provide the description of the action; the second commentator, usually a former player, provides the expert analysis.

There have been some great double acts in recent memory like Miles Harrison and Stuart Barnes on Rugby and David Croft and Martin Brundle in Formula One, David Lloyd and anyone in cricket. The first double act I remember was way back, well before satellite links. It was in boxing on the radio. In those days, the expert second commentator was called 'the cough man'. In other words, he gave the main broadcaster a break, a sip of tea and a chance to get his breath back. An early BBC boxing commentator I remember was Raymond Glendenning, crackling across the airwaves on the old BBC Light Programme. He would describe each round and give way to 'the cough man', W Barrington Dalby, a former boxing referee, to provide his 'inter-round' summary. Glendenning always uttered the words, 'come in, Barry' as the bell sounded for the end of a round. They were a wonderful duo.

The spectacular drama of 'the rumble in the jungle' in Kinshasha, Zaire, in 1974, produced an unforgettable piece of commentary from Harry Carpenter. It was the match for the World Heavyweight Crown between the formidable, forbidding, and unbeaten George Foreman and 'The Greatest' Muhammad Ali on the comeback trail. The humid conditions were draining, and by round eight, both fighters were looking absolutely shattered in the stifling heat.

'Suddenly Ali looks very tired indeed. In fact, Ali, at times now, looks as though he can barely lift his arms up... Oh, he's got him with a right hand! He's got him! Oh, you can't believe it. And I don't think Foreman's going to get up. He's trying to beat the count. And he's out! OH MY GOD he's won the title back at thirty-two! Muhammad Ali!'

Ali had trained specifically to take a lot of Foreman's big punches to the arms and torso, although he was dazed at times, but was depending on Foreman burning himself out in the pressure cooker conditions. Carpenter's commentary is a commanding use of short and punchy (excuse the unintended pun) sentences that really get across the frantic nature of the event. It was one of sport's most legendary contests, with Ali a four to one outsider on the night. The commentary really added to the pictures and emphasized the drama as the mighty Foreman was toppled by the cunning Ali.

Like most great commentators, Harry Carpenter did his research and homework, so he knew everything about the two opponents. When covering any team sport, it is a good idea to have a summary of all the players on a screen or note pad in front of you. Just a basic synopsis will be okay. You do not need to know what they have for breakfast or the name of their pet Great Dane. However, it could be of interest. A quick resume like this is useful.

GEORGE JONES. Striker. Age 23. Height 5 foot 8 inches. Joined 2019 from Cowdenbeath on a free transfer. Forty-three games and fourteen goals. Never scored from outside the penalty area. Started training as a lion tamer in a circus before going into football. He was spotted in a Sunday League game in Wick.

When commentating on sport, there is always a tendency for hyperbole, getting excited and overstating and exaggerating like this.

'Wow. Amazing. That was truly the most spectacular event in the history of the sport, Stan.'

'I would have to say, history of the world, Dick.'

Those were the comments on Stenhousemuir's comeback from two goals down to beat Stirling Albion.

Another pitfall in commentary is to 'lag behind'. I once heard a commentator saying, 'and the ball is with Brown on the halfway line', and as he said it, there were roars as a goal was scored. He had a little catching up to do.

It can be very tricky when you are commentating on a team you support and cannot be partisan. Do not be biased or too opinionated. Remember, it is a commentary. Ask yourself, 'is what I have said fair and accurate?' If your team wins, try to be neutral and keep celebrations under wraps until you are out of sight. Do not jump about in jubilation on the gantry or in the press box.

One of the most interesting prospects about live commentaries and broadcasts is the location. For most sport events, a broadcaster commentates from a gantry which is a raised platform, usually looking over the halfway line and often built into or on top of the main stand. Most seem to be under the rafters. A piece of equipment that should be compulsory for commentators as PPE (personal protective equipment) would be a hard hat or crash helmet. There are plenty of hazards to negotiate.

Notts County once had a gantry that was a flat platform at the top of their old creaking stand. The ascent was like scaling the north face of the Eiger. Our crew had to negotiate a series of ladders with those protective hoops around. Not much attention to health and safety in those days. I felt obliged to help the camera operator by carrying up a piece of equipment like a tripod. This usually meant catching my head on part of the ladder or equipment and having an even chance of suffering from concussion before reaching the summit of the commentary point.

Once on the top, it was a fabulous view, but the platform was completely open to the elements from all sides. The wind, rain, sleet and snow whistled in from every direction. No protection whatsoever. For one fixture on a night when the temperature fell well below freezing, and the pitch was covered in snow, to everyone's surprise, the match went ahead. The snow was rolled flat to provide insulation to stop the ground underneath from freezing, coloured lines were painted, and a bright orange ball was used. The game was a complete farce. Afterwards, some of the players complained of having 'burns' from sliding about on the ice and snow. I have never been so cold in my life. I was numb and sat in the car with the heater full on for about half an hour before I could get the feeling back in my fingers and toes. Peterborough United also used to have a camera point where we were open to arctic conditions on a cold winter's day. A flat asphalt plateau, with penetrating winds hitting us from all sides.

There were many challenging gantries that would have tested Sherpa Tensing or Bear Grylls. At Anfield, back in the 1980s, it was an extraordinary trek upstairs and along parapets to reach the point high up on the stand. Nottingham Forest had a long, boarded walkway to the gantry, which had an obstacle course of low steel girders to duck under. Another head injury hazard.

At Queens Park Rangers, the gantry used to be 'a steel cage'. Not exactly expedient for insulation against the chill and another location where I nearly suffered from exposure. Many fans will remember when the club became one of the first to utilise an all-weather plastic pitch. One that was very controversial as the bounce was so high. But the surface meant that a match could be played whatever the weather. One Saturday afternoon with sub-zero temperatures, QPR's match went ahead despite a big freeze all over the country. The problem was the steel cage transported the extreme cold from the soles of your feet and up your body. The effect of the metal floor meant that in quite a short time, it was impossible to feel your feet. They were petrified. This feeling of the 'blood freezing' worked its way up the body. We had to take it in turns to run on the spot in the cage to get the circulation going.

Perhaps my favourite commentary position was 'the boat' at the old Twickenham Ground. It was quite literally like a wooden boat tacked on to the side of the main stand. The position was superb. The only worry was we were suspended from the side of the stand. If the floorboards were suffering from a little woodworm or dry rot, the boat crew could have fallen through to the crowd below.

Talking of Rugby, if you commentate on the sport, it is necessary to be able to interpret what is going on at scrum time.

Best of luck with that. It is simple in Rugby League. There are no contested scrums. Since the 1990s an accepted convention or armistice has been introduced so that players do not battle for the ball. The scrum is simply a way to restart the game. With six big forwards packed down, the theory is, it does give the backs a better chance to run a move. I love watching Rugby League, but I wish the sport would go back to pushing in scrums or get rid of the device altogether and find some alternative.

Now, as for Rugby Union scrums, they can be a commentator's confusion. There is so much going on between sixteen players you could throw a blanket over. At most scrums, there can be several players bending the rules. Who is collapsing? Who is boring in at an angle? Who is not bound properly? Whose head has popped up? etc, etc. In that density of wrestling and shoving bodies, it is sometimes impossible to pick out a wrongdoer, even for the referee standing over them.

I really enjoy watching scrums. The power allied to technical skills is awesome and compelling. A problem occurs when we get a succession of them. This seems to happen too frequently in international games. After a scrum has been reset three or four times, several minutes have passed by, cutting down time for the flowing, running play we all like to witness. Scrums and lineouts are a good spectacle and integral to the game, but not many fans want to watch a series of set plays that take up a huge proportion of the match time.

Before the start of a commentary or live broadcast, there is usually the obligatory sound check. Many people just count to ten; others state what they had for breakfast. One excellent radio football commentator I worked with in my formative years in Leeds used to read out a shopping list. The technician or studio assistant would come over to him before the game to hear the list and adjust the sound level for the broadcast.

'Over to you Doug.'

'Yes, two pounds of potatoes, a pound of sprouts, a packet of Daz, four tins of Pedigree Chum and a dozen eggs.'

'Thank you, that is fine for level.'

That is how the sound balance usually happened, but on one afternoon, the technician forgot to carry out a check, and the programme presenter went straight to the match preview at Elland Road, which went something like this ...

'Thank you, two pounds of carrots, four cans of baked beans, Fairy Liquid, two packets of Cornflakes, a block of lard ....'

And so, the match preview went on. Those in the studio were too convulsed with laughter, and the shopping list continued for a time before someone told Doug to wrap up. Most listeners were hoping to get the team news, but this was much more entertaining. The most bizarre match preview ever heard.

Here is another party game involving commentary. A little exercise that is a fun activity to play at home or in the pub. Try to give a shot-by-shot, blow-by-blow account on a tennis match that is on TV. You will be surprised how difficult it is to avoid getting tongue-tied. If you can do that, then you may have some sort of chance of becoming a commentator. It could become a great game, recording a few people after a little light refreshment.

I always tried to remember to take a 'comfort break' before any long live broadcast. Early in my career, I was the sports editor at BBC Radio Leicester. I also presented the breakfast show for a while. The Radio station staff were invited to take part in a skittles match against the local police force. It turned out to be a fun evening, and after the match, there was a serving of lashings of faggots and peas. Faggots were a local delicacy rather like a meatball. They were typically made up of pig's hearts, livers and fatty belly meat. This event was in my first few weeks in Leicester. I had never sampled faggots before.

After the skittles, food and a few beers, I got to bed quite late and had only a couple of hours sleep before getting up at five a.m. to stagger in and present the breakfast show. The programme started at six thirty and was a typical mix of music, chat, local and national news. After settling into the studio chair, I was aware of some strange gurgling sounds emanating from deep down in my stomach. A few minutes later, I was in a bit of pain and felt extremely bloated. I needed to get to the toilet pronto. But it was down the corridor from the studio. So, I put on a long record of over four minutes and struggled with buttocks tightly clenched on a journey to the loo. Montezuma, or more likely those accursed faggots had their revenge. I made it back to the studio with seconds to spare, and the studio technician was looking a little relieved; indeed, so was I, in more ways than one.

I resumed the program, but thirty minutes later, the same emergency happened again. This time I was better rehearsed. I played a long, taped interview. Limped to the loo and returned just in time. I had to make another visit before the end of the programme. I have not eaten faggots since!

There are other live performances you may undertake, especially after dinner speaking or opening various events. These can be extremely hard work, depending on the audience. Very often, at a dinner, you are obliged to sit through a tasteless meal of rubbery chicken – why is it always chicken? Then there is the polite and often contrived conversation with people. At about eleven o'clock, feeling fatigued and wanting to go home, you have to perform, 'give it your all', and produce an entertaining speech.

I was once engaged to be 'the turn' at a working men's club in the Midlands. It really was a huge hall. I could hardly see across the massive space, owing to the thick fog of cigarette smoke. There was table after table of punters with pints of lager and glasses of German white wine, shrouded in the thick mist.

The chairman of the club insisted he would introduce me. He checked my name, and I reiterated that I was Dennis Coath from ITV. About ten o'clock, with the audience well oiled, I was summoned to appear. I waited behind a curtain to the side of the stage and the chairman, wearing a very stark ginger toupee, waddled up to the microphone to do the intro. 'Here he is from the BBC and ITV… Derek Crouch.'

I looked around to see if Derek Crouch was going to make an appearance from the other side of the stage, then the chairman glanced in my direction and beckoned. At that point, I realised that I was now Derek Crouch.

Luckily, I managed to keep my new nom de plume secret; otherwise, my colleagues at work would have had a field day.

Personality profile

There is a lot of difference between a long in-depth interview for a feature and a quick chat standing up for a short quote or sound bite. Nowadays, it is getting harder to carry out a thorough head-to-head with a major sporting personality or to write, record or produce a piece or article of some substance. Too often, the only access to sport stars is via a sterile press conference, with a background of irritating advert boards and a room full of various reporters. The other option is often that snatched chat which could be rushed and restricted. Just getting access can be problematic as some stars only do business through their agent, an intermediary, or press officer. There are also those who demand a fee. That may be okay if they are going out of their way to take part in a media feature. But if not, in my opinion, it can be very selfish, as they have a fan base who want to hear from them.

There is, of course, the obvious question. How do you define a personality? As in many walks of life, some sport competitors can be very bland and uninteresting. For a lengthy feature, you really need a subject who has something powerful, witty, or interesting to say and who is ebullient in their speech and body language. The sort of person who is compelling and makes you want to sit up and listen.

The three most interesting people I have interviewed who fit into this category were not sport stars. They were the comedian

Ken Dodd, naturalist David Attenborough and music legend Rod Stewart. They provided the three 'Fs' – fascinating, forthcoming and fun. I did not have to work hard with this trio to record some brilliant material. Doddy and David were live chats and could have held the attention of listeners for hours. Hardly a sentence was dull or wasted. Rod Stewart was a recorded interview and extremely entertaining. On each occasion, there would have been enough excellent stuff for several features.

So, I go back to my original question, who is a personality? By the way you conduct the interview and use the material, you can make people even more engrossing; but first, why do you want to do a personality profile?

It may be to preview a big event or to publicise a new revelation. It might be to explore a new aspect of their life. The subject could be involved in a major issue, or it could be much simpler – a big star is available for a chat.

There has been a trend for famous sport stars to publish autobiographies early in their lives, then bring out others as their career develops. Wayne Rooney's first book came out when he was just twenty. It was aptly titled, 'My Story So Far'. Others have followed a similar approach.

What makes for an interesting chat to a sport star? Many factors contribute to their persona. What makes them tick? You may want to draw out the characteristics that create their courage and will to win. We want to know what makes a 'champion'? It can be an interesting study to examine a day in the life of a personality. What are their training and preparation like? Stories of triumph over adversity are nearly always compelling. There are also other aspects to their lives outside of sport. In fact, their general outlook on life can reveal a few titbits.

But what the reader, listener or viewer really wants is a chat that is perceptive and intuitive. Am I being told things I did not know? This is fascinating; I am really getting inside the mind of the subject. I feel I am learning his or her inner secrets and getting an idea about what makes them perform. That was a searching insight. I now feel I really know the person!

Further depth to a profile can be gained by talking to "significant others". Possible interviewees would be parents, wives, husbands, coaches, teachers, managers and fans. This approach could amplify any feature on a top sport star.

Extracting something really revealing is always very satisfying. When conducting an interview, notice the best quotes as the conversation progresses. I am a big fan of twenty-times champion National Hunt Jockey Tony or A.P. McCoy. Before his achievement, I would have said that winning a score of those titles was impossible. If you bear in mind the intensity of the number of rides in a year, plus the burden of injuries, it is one of the greatest sporting feats of all time. In his career A.P. broke a leg, arm, ankle, wrists, shoulder, collar bones, cheekbones, vertebrae and all his ribs. He also suffered from punctured lungs and many broken teeth. I was indebted to him for riding some unlikely winners. I remember one McCoy winner I backed at Ludlow. The horse was back in the pack and looked to have no chance, but A.P. appeared to almost lift it, coax, and power it home as though it had suddenly developed afterburners. A.P. could be severely bashed and bruised after a fall and simply ignore the pain and ride a winner in the next race. If a jockey is prostrate on the turf after a bad fall and feels completely numb, there is a fear that the rider has suffered serious injury, like a broken back. McCoy admitted that he only had one thought going through his mind. That was not, 'am I paralysed'? But 'how soon can I get back on a horse'? It is sheer bloody-mindedness and determination.

He also had developed what could be described as a 'failure phobia'. McCoy once stated, *'you dream about being champion jockey, and then champion jockey again. The fear of failure is always there. The more you win, the more you fear not winning. And that's when I'll retire. Maybe I am obsessed.'* An incredible champ who perhaps revealed a little insecurity with his addiction to winning.

In chats with great sport stars, there is a theme – a desire for invincibility. 'I hate to lose', Jessica Ennis-Hill said of her Olympic Gold Heptathlon victory, which was completed when she hit the tape first in the eight-hundred-metres race. *'When they came back at me, I thought, damn! But I wanted to cross that line first, even though I didn't need to win the race. Why? You train all year for one moment, so what's the point in easing down? You give it everything, leave it all on the track.'*

An in-depth interview should be just that. The conversation may extract some fascinating thoughts from the subject. To conduct a long interview, it is necessary to engage, enthuse and empathise. Work out a strategy and a series of questions. Do not stick too rigidly to the plan, as the interview may go in an unexpected and fascinating direction. Your job is to guide it. If possible, do not sit with a note pad, tablet, mobile phone or clipboard on your lap and refer to it. That can be distracting to your subject. They may feel at a disadvantage. In fact, try not to have any object between you and the person you are chatting to, apart from a microphone. Engage with eye contact, and try and be warm, even if the chat is challenging. Body language is also important so try to be relaxed. This applies even if it is a hostile interview. Anyone looks and reasons better if they are calm and polite, not angry. Do research and homework and have all the information 'in your head'.

The key aspect of any personality profile is to carry out a good warm-up before you start to record anything. The idea is to put the interviewee at their ease and get a rapport going, so you start off at full speed rather than idling. With some the preliminaries are easy, I will use Ken Dodd, David Attenborough, and Rod Stewart as examples.

Ken needed no easing into it. He was the epitome of the 'showbiz pro'. No warm-up was needed, as he was on top form from the start. It was a case of switch him on and let him go! I have never heard such a stream of great jokes, stories, and recollections before, that have been so engrossing and enjoyable. He stayed for the full two hours of the radio show, and I have rarely been so enthralled and entertained. The performance was amazing. Trying to remember all the gags was impossible. He and Peter Kay are my top stand-ups of all time.

Before the interview with David Attenborough, we talked about his earliest series, the Zoo Quest Expeditions. It was my favourite TV show as a child. I watched it in glorious black and white and avidly read the book about the expeditions to South America. I could remember all the stories. So, we had the perfect introduction to the interview.

With Rod Stewart, it was again an interesting chatty process. We had both grown up in the same area of London and remembered gigs we had been to. He is also a fanatical football man and had trials with Brentford, and of course, he is an avid Scotland fan. We had plenty in common; the warm-up and chat virtually merged into one after the gig, refreshed by large glasses of brandy and cola.

A good way to help the introduction is to do research on the guest to identify some areas in common, like similar hobbies or interests. It may be that you both come from the same town, have children of the same age, play a lot of golf, or, best of all, support the same football team.

One of my most engaging subjects was the former World Motor Racing Champion Alain Prost. I have interviewed him twice at racing circuits. On both occasions I approached him in the pits, and he said very politely, 'come along to my motor home in about twenty minutes, and I will be ready.' When I arrived with the camera crew at his sumptuous portable pad, Alain was sat outside, relaxing in the sunshine. In front of him was a big tray of freshly brewed coffee and delicious biscuits. If there is one thing a camera crew appreciates, it is complimentary refreshments. A few years ago, an average TV crew could make a flock of vultures look a bit picky. Alain was the perfect host and a great chatter. His English was immaculate. The coffee and biscuits helped to make for a very congenial conversation.

When there is someone in front of you to converse for a good length of time, you can really draw out interesting answers. Try not to ask closed questions. It is an old journalistic maxim. Start off questions with – how, who, what, when, where and why? Other methods to really extract information are lines like… 'describe to me' or 'outline how' or 'tell me about'.

The other advantage for a long conversation is, it is possible to probe and get a key question answered. For example, I had to interview a football club chairman after a relegation campaign during the recession of 2007 to 2009. There were rumours of big staff cuts. I posed the same question, couched slightly differently, three times before I got a satisfactory answer. The same tactic is frequently used by political journalists talking to evasive politicians trying to dodge the question. My three questions were something along the lines of.

'You've got three hundred employees. How will you be affected in the current recession?'

'How will cutbacks hit jobs at this organisation?'

'What would the message be to your workforce in these times of economic stringency?

Do not be afraid to stir up a little indignity. 'Your club has not fared very well in the current recession. You are the Chairman. What are you going to do about it?'

The two questions to ask yourself are… before the interview. 'Is the subject relaxed and ready to go?'… After the chat, 'have I got a right, riveting article or recording?'

The worst possible scenario with a personality profile is when you have a top celebrity ready for a chat, and there is a subject concerning them that is the 'hot topic', and they are not prepared to talk about it. You are doing the introductory stuff and say something like, 'we'll talk about your days at Madrid, how your move back to the Premiership is shaping up and chat about your England career.'

Then you probe and add a little rider in as diplomatic a tone as you can muster, 'look, while you are here, can we chat about your boyhood addiction to glue sniffing, talk about those recent pictures of you snorting cocaine in Kew Gardens, your affair with the Duchess of Cockfosters and those dogging expeditions in Windsor Great Park? I know this may be difficult, but you have a chance to tell your side of the story.'

At this point, it is quite within the bounds of possibility that you may get a flat 'NO', and your interviewee proves rather reticent to talk about the improprieties. 'I am not going to talk about any of this, just do not ask me.' Oh dear, you have probably only lined up the chat to talk about the scandals. That can be very disappointing. It is often better for the celebrity to be honest, tell the story and maybe apologise to fans. In that way, conjecture is flattened to a certain extent, otherwise the story becomes a long-running piece of theory, speculation, gossip and guesswork.

Rolling News

Our lives have been changed forever by 'twenty-four-hour news' or 'rolling news'. It even applies to newspapers that run up-to-the-minute websites. There are now many rolling news services on radio, websites and TV, with new ones springing up every year. Stories require constant changing and updating. Editors and correspondents are continually asking, 'what is the next and the next and the next development of the event or story?' This has always been the natural inquisitive instinct since early man and was aided by the first printing press invented by Johannes Gutenburg in 1450. It applies to anyone, even those spilling out a story or piece of local gossip to friends. 'Have you heard about the Johnsons?' 'Fancy that, and with him as well.' 'And he's old enough to be her father.' But the big question on the local bush telegraph and national media networks is, 'what happened next?' That is the basis of twenty-four-hour news.

Rolling news continues to grow in intensity, and the twenty-four-hour channels need to be well-fed with material. Sport news has the biggest appetite with those continuing sagas like football transfer stories or managerial sackings. Before the advent of these intensive news outlets, people would have to wait a long time for a Radio or TV news bulletin or for the morning or evening newspaper to come out. Now it is instant news, tune in at any hour of the day or night to your favourite TV or Radio station or go to a particular website. In other words, you can choose when you want to check up on news or sport news.

Technology is moving at a rapid rate. Satellite trucks for coverage are now cheap and commonplace. New portable gadgetry means journalists can broadcast live from almost any part of the world with little difficulty. Very soon, a journalist will be sending a TV report from the middle of the Gobi Desert using a piece of kit the size of a baked bean can or a matchbox.

My first real experience of rolling news in its infancy was back in 1973 when I covered the tragic Lofthouse Colliery Pit disaster, in which seven men died after being trapped underground. It was an extremely sad and grim affair. I was a news trainee at BBC Radio Leeds, and my instrument to provide an infusion of up-dates into the news bulletins was 'ye olde radio car'. It was a proud Cortina estate with a telescopic aerial that projected out of the roof. This was the ancestor of modern satellite trucks.

The rescue mission took six days, and I was stationed at the pit head for most of the time. I even slept in the radio car one night. Every day I had to find a new story or angle. One report I compiled was about the incredibly brave rescue teams, who would do a long shift underground and work until they were exhausted. They came to the surface, collapsed in a blanket and after a quick shower, mug of tea, and a bacon sandwich were ready to go again. The rescue teams were both amazing and heroic! I did a story about the vigil of the waiting relatives and one about a power drill. It was hoped this contraption would bore through the earth and rock to reach the trapped men, but it proved to be a false hope.

I did not dare leave the colliery for a moment in case I missed anything for my broadcasts. The only food and refreshments that were constantly available were those big mugs of tea and bacon sarnies. They were addictive, but after four or five days on this exclusive bread, brew and bacon diet and little chance to bathe or shower, I smelt like a transport café. The radio car was the first instant vehicle for continuous reports. My work earned a commendation from the National Coal Board.

The wavelength wagon worked very well until one reporter drove the car home with the aerial still up and snapped it off, trying to get into his garage. The vehicle was out of commission for several weeks, while a new antenna was fitted with a control that meant the engine would not start if you tried to drive with the aerial erected.

In a more recent experience of rolling news, I could relate that if you are reporting from a location for the day, try to choose a pleasant place. I covered a national dustbin workers strike and was stationed by a big depot in the Midlands. Our site was an endless line of big crammed, stinking bins, about fifty yards long and fifty yards wide. I was stuck by the dustbins all day with barely a thirty-minute break. 'Bins to the left of me, bins to the right. Here I am, stuck in the middle…' My first live report was for the morning news bulletin. Now I would admit to a phobia about rats. I would rather face a raging bull elephant or grizzly bear after nicking a salmon sandwich from his picnic basket. Rats are the most appalling creatures in the animal kingdom, Ugh! Just as I was about to utter my first words on the report, a huge, bedraggled rat crawled out of the top of the bin I was leaning against. I sounded a little tense and edgy, especially when I heard more rustling sounds behind me. I spent the rest of the day reporting from the line of bins, getting used to the repulsive, rotting odour, petrified that 'king rat' would reappear.

I wonder if someone secretly had it in for me as I seem to have presented outside broadcasts from some revolting places. While working on the news for ITV in Birmingham, we had a tip-off from the police and health officials that a consignment of chicken, well past its sell-by date, was about to be sent out on the market. The officials had seized the meat, which was laid out in a warehouse. This was not just a few wings and legs, but masses of chicken parts in containers, filling a large hall. The chicken was coated in mould and bespattered with faeces. I was careful not to take a deep breath, as I would have thrown up. The stench was stifling and revolting. If the contents of the warehouse had not been intercepted and the perpetrators arrested, the meat would have been cleaned up with bleach and sent out to local shops and restaurants. If the smell was not bad enough, I had to pick up some of the worst pieces of flesh and show them to the camera. It was a big relief to wash my hands thoroughly and get out into the fresh air without vomiting. It is sobering to think, without good intelligence from health inspectors and prompt action from the police, that chicken would have appeared on some restaurant dinner plates or in some Sunday lunches.

Sport stories provide excellent fodder for twenty-four-hour news. Waiting on a new manager to be appointed by a top Premiership club is always a protracted process that needs a succession of live updates; there is plenty of speculation. My favourite rumour is the spurious reports of candidates being seen in estate agents. That nearly always crops up. It is somewhat amusing, 'so and so was spotted today in Fiddler, Capone and Crooks, looking at property in the area.' A close watch is maintained at the ground and training facility for any significant arrivals. A shortlist is supposedly drawn up. Then various prospective managers are eliminated. All the shenanigans can go on for days or weeks, with reports on the latest situation or speculation.

I remember a couple of days when a horde of the sporting press was encamped outside a ground and restricted to the car park. There was the drama of one manager leaving and another arriving. The problem was the car park was covered in ice and snow, and the outside temperature was about minus five Centigrade. It was not a lot of fun being holed up there for a day. Most of the time, everyone was in their cars with the heater on, waiting for anything to happen. The club had little idea about public relations and could have had the courtesy of providing some hot drinks for the waiting "journos".

As I mentioned before, many sport stories turn into long, never-ending tales of the unexpected or more frequently… expected. The story always needs to be 'freshened up'. The reporter on the scene has a job to provide different lines or angles to bring out, to keep the pot boiling.

There are bound to be plenty of 'egg on face' moments in live broadcasting. That is the nature of the beast. When your first on-air boob happens, you feel very embarrassed. After you have suffered a few, it is like water off a duck's back. With rolling news, it is not quite so much making a mountain out of a molehill but making more out of less. The main concern is that you are 'on the scene', keeping abreast of all the latest developments. A day's live reports about a sporting event can be very exhilarating. It is pleasant to be stationed at a cricket ground watching the play all day, very pleasurable to be at Ascot or Aintree or at a football training ground on a sunny day. Better than standing by a row of rat-infested, rancid, rotten, repulsive dustbins or among a vast collection of putrid, mouldy chicken pieces!

The Press Conference

The news or press conference or 'presser' has become an institution, or even a piece of theatre and is especially significant in sport. We have all witnessed them on television. Everything from the American President's audience with the media to Hayseed Town's weekly news conference in League Two. The standard meeting is used for a weekly discharge of information at football clubs, rugby teams and a few other sport organisations. A one-off, special presser is staged when a club makes a big signing, announces a major financial move, a change in management or any significant happening.

Pressers have improved and are more orderly now. They used to be a bunfight. A verbal crossfire and a bovine stampede. A cacophony of "journos" shouting out questions all at once. There used to be a physical shoving match, too, with reporters and camera crews jostling to get into the best position. It was a bit like a rugby maul with cameras, note books, laptops and voice recorders. In television, it was always an advantage to have an extremely large, battle-hardened, camera crew. Something like the England front row could have been useful, that is, if they could operate cameras and sound. I remember once attending an important presser with a camera operator at six foot two, a soundman at six foot three and an electrician at six foot five. We were able to muscle in at the front to get the best shot and put up a human barrier.

Then there was this extraordinary competition, rather like boxers at the bell straining to throw the first punch, Grand Prix drivers thrusting to get to the front when the lights go out, or characters in westerns itching to be first on the draw. Who could ask the first question? It was a ridiculous situation as sometimes journos would be firing off three separate questions simultaneously. It had got to the point that, as soon as the interviewees were in sight, even before they had sat down, someone was bawling out a question.

It is great to witness that a more sensible organised practice now happens in news conferences. Usually, a designated press officer or media chief guides the event and asks reporters in turn for their questions. The journos usually announce who they are and which media organisation they represent. You wait until you are invited to ask a question. Not so much fun, maybe, but better than the old free for all. It eliminates the larynx straining, shouting match.

Even better news is that at most major pressers, refreshments are laid on. That means the media can display the primeval instincts I mentioned before and act like a plague of locusts or a pack of slobbering Labradors in a cake-eating contest. Not a crumb is left. I was reminded of this scenario when watching a David Attenborough sequence on vultures. I remember in one of the first top football matches I ever covered, a well-known newspaper reporter was holding court in the press room holding a pie in one hand, a sandwich in the other, salivating and spitting out crumbs and pastry. A massive gut was bursting through his braces and hanging over his waist. To be medically accurate, he was grossly obese. I found it extremely irritating, listening to this huge lardy figure criticising svelte athletes.

My greatest irritation in pressers was the reporters who sat silently and did not ask a single question. All they did was scribble down the results of other people's interrogation. Another criticism, as I have mentioned earlier, is quite often, it may be the only occasion you get to interview certain sport stars. I believe fans want to see their favourite personalities in other scenarios away from the football or training ground. Plus, there is also a practice at many football and rugby clubs where they put up just one or two of their staff for interview. Not a subject of your choice. A Premiership club once made available only one player for a Friday conference. He scored only one out of ten on our chat assessment marks. We managed to salvage two five-second clips that were just about usable. It was not exactly edge-of-the-seat stuff.

The weekly presser at a club can also be a bit tedious, especially if little is happening. You often get down to just the injury or casualty list or what is more fondly called 'groin strain news'. Managers will typically say. *'Wayne's got a bit of hamstring. Carlos has been feeling something in his groin. Luigi has a twinge in his head. Willie was told he was getting a cortisone injection today. He was disappointed. He thought it was a high-performance car. Anyway, I expect them all to be fit for Saturday.'*

Oh great, hold the front page. Some managers see pressers as a tedious duty, but there are others who can conduct or almost compere a very amusing session. There is also a small minority who can turn a presser into a cabaret.

Many football clubs have now started laying on excellent refreshments for their press conferences. This is a very welcome experience. I wondered why camera crews were so keen to cover the 'presser' at West Bromwich Albion every Friday, especially as the manager at that time held the meeting first thing in the morning. I soon found out. The club laid on tureens of eggs, bacon, sausages, tomatoes, toast and mushrooms, followed by Danish pastries and hot beverages. It was not so much the big breakfast but the morning banquet. I felt like going to sleep for the rest of the day. By contrast, another club had just an awful coffee machine for press conferences which served up a brew that tasted like a mix of gravy and motor fuel.

One of the worst catering experiences I suffered at a big press event was during a semi-final in one of the major one-day cricket competitions. The day was sponsored by a big national company. In the press box, we were delighted to be presented with a little picnic hamper at lunchtime. On opening it, we were less than delighted. It comprised of a miniature, warm bottle of white wine and a curled-up cheese sandwich. But there was at least a pork pie. I was the first to bite through the pie and swallowed half of it very quickly as I was ravenous. I looked at the remaining section in my hand and noticed many new strains of penicillin. The filling was mainly a kind of blue mould. Luckily for the others, I had acted as the guinea pig, and they chucked their pies in the bin. I went to a nearby bar and swallowed two neat vodkas, which luckily seemed to kill off any bugs, and I got through the rest of the day without any upset.

I could not do that!

It is always fascinating, compelling, and awe-inspiring to cover a sport which makes you think, 'I could not do that!' It is an excellent starting point to produce or write a profile on a competitor in an event in which you consider the courage needed, as well as the technique. Many of us probably dream that with a little, or quite a lot, more talent, we could be footballers, cricketers, golfers, tennis stars, athletes, hockey, or netball players, etc.

But ask yourself, 'what event would I find the most frightening?' How about going into a boxing ring, riding a horse over a steeplechase course like Aintree, playing in the front row of a rugby scrum, and piloting a MotoGP bike? No thanks! Another activity I have added to the 'no go' category is the exhausting triathlon. I could also add pole vaulting, ice hockey, bob sleighing, downhill skiing, white-water rafting, parachuting, cage fighting and quite a few others. So, I am in complete admiration of individuals who compete in some sports. When you have this approach to a certain activity, it can make for an absorbing feature. Can you conceive what it is like? What aptitude do you need? Apart from voluminous bags of courage. Are you ever scared? I would be bloody terrified. **I could not do that!**

I have enjoyed making a few television features on MotoGP riders like Valentino Rossi and Wayne Gardner. They are a separate breed! The modern bike is 1000cc, and the acceleration is frightening. They go from 0 to 100mph in 2.2 seconds. The top speed can theoretically reach 390kph, which is 242mph. Riders have topped 220mph in Grand Prix. It is just like being perched on a rocket supported by two thin bands of rubber. I remember one top competitor telling me that only a very few riders were really qualified to ride these delicately tuned bikes. MotoGP riders display subtle control as there is little room for error; they also need to be lithe and possess gymnastic ability on the twitchy machines. Judgement needs to be spot on. The riders are super-fit and display unbreakable concentration. One tiny mistake can lead to injury or a disaster. It is also incredible to watch spills on the track from which competitors get up virtually unscathed. As well as amazing performers, MotoGP produces remarkable personalities as well.

Valentino Rossi was the most daredevil rider I have ever seen. Marc Marquez is also brilliant. Rossi really pushed himself and his machine to the limits and won nine world titles as a result. He once held court for a few reporters on a riverboat chugging up and down the Thames. Valentino is a thoroughly engaging character, and it was an excellent and ever-changing backdrop for a chat. He came up with many great lines in the conversation. My favourite was that to relax, he said he liked to ride a motorbike around the North Circular Road. A sort of busman's holiday, I suppose. Just imagine if he was pulled over by the police for speeding. 'Who do you think you are, Valentino Rossi?'

In the chapter about personality profiles, I mentioned the extraordinary twenty times Champion National Hunt jockey Tony McCoy. Events like the Cheltenham Gold Cup and the Grand National are exciting spectacles; but can you imagine the courage, technique and astuteness needed to become a top jump jockey? Galloping down to that first fence at Aintree must be absolutely nerve-tingling, a cure for constipation! The only certainty for a jump jockey is you are going to break some bones. There was a recent survey that calculated a jump jockey had a fall every twenty rides, and in twenty-five per cent of cases the spill will result in an injury. It is a sobering fact, but these results are a great improvement on the fate of National Hunt riders even a few years ago. Protective gear and medical support have improved beyond all measure. We are now getting many jump jockeys still competing past the age of forty. Four-time champion Richard Johnson and Barry Geraghty are two top-notch jockeys who rode on past two score years. They must be gluttons for punishment or have a high pain threshold. For many accomplished riders, the thought of four, five or six races in a day at a typical meeting would be daunting.

Rugby is supposed to be a game for people of all shapes and sizes. Shapes may differ, but nowadays, you must be a largish unit to play in any position. There are few players in the professional and international game who weigh under thirteen stone. High protein diets and scientific weight training have greatly increased muscle bulk. In the England team of 1953, the tight-head prop, often the heftiest player in the side, tipped the scales at twelve stone and eight pounds! In the 1960s the famous French half backs, the Camberabero twins, were real lightweights. Outside half Guy weighed just over ten stone and scrum half, Lilian, not much over nine stone. Even the greatest ever half back pairing of Gareth Edwards and Barry John of Wales were comparative lightweights at under twelve stone. Modern scrum halves can now be over fourteen stone. Recent Wales number nine Mike Phillips is six foot three and weighs in at nearly sixteen stone. It is hard to take in that Fijian back

Nemani Nadolo is six foot five and twenty-one and a half stone… and he is a winger. They used to be whippet-like creatures not so long ago.

If you are in the front row of the scrum, you are likely to be built like a brick outhouse. There are now some international prop forwards who tip the scales at over twenty stone and are surprisingly mobile. Even hookers often reach eighteen stone or more. The combined weight of a scrum is usually not far off a ton. So just envisage the force when two packs lock horns? It is two moving masses of flesh, bone and muscle pushing and crunching against one another. The utmost in crushing power. What is it like to be in the middle as a prop forward or hooker? A No-Go Area! It must be exacting and exhausting, to say the least. The pressure on the neck must be extreme. These are positions I could not remotely imagine playing in. Prop forwards have assured me it is simply a matter of technique. If you are taught correctly, there should not be a problem. There is though, the proviso that you need to be at least seventeen stone, immensely strong, with legs like concrete bollards, a big collar size and nowadays the ability to carry the ball and make yardage. It is a sporting position in which there is plenty of guile used, as well as beef and brawn; but props have also told me, that to be a hooker, you must be mad!

There is an old sporting saying the boxing ring is 'the loneliest place in the world'. Contemplate sitting in a corner, and the bell goes and coming across the ring towards you is someone like Marvelous Marvin Hagler, Sugar Ray Leonard or Mike Tyson. The stuff of nightmares. You are on your own; there is no one else to help you. I would run for it and not look back or get the corner to throw the towel in as soon as the bell sounded. The dedication, training and fitness required to be a world champion boxer is off the scale. Fitness levels are extraordinary. After all, you are preparing for a contest in which your opponent is aiming to knock your block off. The oldest adage is, 'you need to hit and not be hit'. That all sounds fine in theory. When you see the power of the punches thrown and the rapidity of the combinations from great fighters, it is a bit awe-inspiring.

I was lucky enough to interview Marvelous (the one L is the American spelling!) Marvin Hagler. In my opinion one of the greatest pound-for-pound pugilists of all time. Marvin had an extraordinarily long reach and threw vicious punches from all sorts of angles. He was also able to switch hit. He could change his stance many times during a fight if he wished. Menacing in the ring and mannerly out of it, he was very amusing. He did give me some advice. My hair was disappearing fast, and he suggested I should shave my skull like him. Great advice; I have been doing it ever since. Thanks for that, Marvin.

I have reported on many boxing events and produced features on several top boxers. As a teenager, I watched all the Muhammad Ali fights on television, never dreaming I would meet and interview him. I recorded a radio interview with him in the 1970s. Then I recall talking to him for a TV feature in the 1990s when Parkinson's Syndrome had started to take effect; his speech was slow and more deliberate, but he was still mentally sharp, witty and, after his boxing career, did not appear to have a blemish or scar on his face. He was still the greatest and the prettiest! It was almost unreal to sit or stand in front of one of the biggest names of the twentieth century and not feel humbled.

As his story unfolded in the 1960s, there would be a report on the radio the morning after his latest fight, and then the contest was shown in glorious black and white in the evening in Britain. At school, we were enthralled by his theatrical exploits and all his brilliant talk and one-liners. I followed his career as he progressed to be the world champion after two dramatic wins over the feared Sonny Liston. Our special favourite was when he said he was going to give someone 'a whuppin'. It became part of our language, if we won at any school sport. 'We gave them a whuppin.' That still applies today, even if I win at Scrabble.

Motorbike racing, National Hunt racing, the front row of the scrum and boxing are daunting. As for the triathlon, people deserve a medal just for taking part. The long swim of one and a half kilometres would be lung bursting. That done, get out of the water and with no time to dry down properly, check your tyres are pumped up, get on the bike, and pedal like you are being chased by a pack of hungry wolves. That ride of a mere forty kilometres must be gruelling, but you have not finished yet. Time to change into running shoes and compete in a ten kilometre race... bloody hellfire!

What could be worse than that ordeal? The answer would be the Ironman Triathlon! It starts with a swim of just under four kilometres, followed by a cycle ride of around one hundred and eighty kilometres and ends with a full marathon. Who thought that up, the Marquis de Sade, Genghis Khan, Torquemada or Ivan the Terrible? That is not so much in the **I could not do that** department; but **'you must be bloody kidding!'**

The only part of the triathlon I have carried out is a long run. They have a saying in the army, 'never volunteer'; advice I should have heeded. I agreed to film a feature on running a marathon. The race I took part in was the Nottingham 'Robin Hood Marathon'. I produced a feature on the preparation and build-up to the event. So, I was theoretically ready for the challenge. I had competed in cross-country and what was then the 880 yards at school. That was a long time ago, and the marathon was a good bit longer.

I settled down to a comfortable jog over the first mile but then witnessed a runner pegged out by an ambulance with a series of wires and tubes attached. A not very comforting sight. There are many mistakes a competitor can make in taking on a marathon. One of the keys is to take in constant *sips* of water so you absorb it. My big error was to glug down too much. I was like a runaway water butt, with the excess liquid sloshing about in my stomach. Another fact many do not realise is that the last few miles are much harder than the previous twenty or so. I reached seventeen miles and was feeling pretty good. The water was still slopping around. But I was okay. Over the next few miles, I started to get stomach cramps, tight leg muscles and began expelling some of the water. The last four miles were agony. I passed some spectators, and a man confronted me and said, 'you are only doing this because you are on telly.' I had just enough energy left to either punch the bloke or struggle to the finish. I chose the latter.

The last three miles seemed to take longer than the previous twenty-three. I was relieved to see the finish, but with every small stride it seemed to recede into the distance. Eventually, I made it. The race was sponsored by Pork Farms, and as each runner passed the finish, they were presented with a pork pie. My first reaction was to throw up that tank of water I had been carrying around. After running over twenty-six miles, suffering from sickness, stomach and muscle cramps, the last thing I wanted to see was a pork pie.

I completed the course in three hours and twenty-two minutes, but with much better experience, I recorded three hours and eight minutes for the London Marathon. It took over three minutes to get through to the start line. Then there was another hold up I did not bargain for. In the dense crowd of runners, it was impossible to do more than a slow jog over the first three miles. I would have come in under three hours had it not been for those problems. That is my story, and I am sticking to it. I felt wrecked for the next few days after the marathons, so what do people feel like after completing a triathlon?

Sacred Cows

This is the most difficult concept in journalism. It is always a moot point for deliberations. You have got to make a choice at the time and often a snap decision. Have you taken the right option? I can only help a little and offer some sort of guidance. It is up to you.

The plain fact is that there are no 'sacred cows' in journalism. If a government official is accused of embezzlement, a football manager has been creaming off transfer funds, or an athletics chief has instructed competitors to take drugs, you will obviously publish the story, provided of course it is accurate and legally watertight. It is in the interests of the public that you write or broadcast the facts. It really does not matter if the perpetrator of these misdemeanours is a close friend, world-famous star, or good contact. People have a right to know the truth! You have a duty to put out the story.

In general news this is nearly always the case. There are no sacred cows. Having established that, I am now going to cause some confusion and contradiction by saying it is not always that clear-cut. There are occasions, especially in sport journalism, when you may calculate you are going to benefit by not putting out a certain story. These decisions are difficult. Damned if you do, damned if you don't. It is hard to advise anyone how to approach these situations. You really need to weigh up the pros and cons.

To give an example, when I was a young radio reporter, I witnessed a training ground punch-up. Skirmishes, and set-tos are not uncommon in training or even in the tunnel after a match. I have seen plenty of them. Usually, they look like something out of a Chuckle Brothers act or a Vic and Bob sketch. There is a lot of pushing, jostling, bawling, and shouting, but most of the punches connect with air. On this occasion, two players had been niggling each other during a six-a-side match, and one swung a big right-hand haymaker that landed flush on the chin. The upshot was his teammate suffered from a broken jaw and was out of action for a few weeks. The manager immediately took me to one side and suggested I had not seen anything. My initial thoughts were that it was not a great story. As a radio reporter, I had no actuality and no interview material to back up the happening. It would just be a voice piece, with my account of the set-to. Plus the fact that, as I mentioned, training ground brawls were commonplace. Another factor was I happened to be the only press person to witness the scrap. If other journalists had been present, I would have reported on the fight. So, I calculated it would be in my best interests to keep schtum about the incident. It turned out to be a sound piece of diplomacy. The next week the club made a record sale, and the manager tipped me off about the story. Keeping the fight off the back pages proved to be a good piece of horse-trading. I had built up trust with a manager who was now very forthcoming with future stories.

This kind of scenario is torturous when you are the reporter on a patch and depend on the football club for regular info. You need to build up a relationship to produce written or broadcast material. It is a difficult operation; there should not be any 'sacred cows' but… you will have to decide for yourself.

Extras, Gripes and Groans

One of the biggest challenges is keeping up with the increasing list of minority sports. A few have faded away. We used to have rope climb, pistol duelling and club swinging in the Olympics. Events like synchronised swimming and beach volleyball are now well established but do not fret; there are plenty of novel activities on the way.

New sports to watch out for include, Hammerfield, Supa Punt and Blo Ball. Hammerfield was inspired by the film 'the Avengers'. Very basically, it is full contact, with two teams of eight, comprising four hammer bearers and four soldiers. You score by throwing a hammer at the goal or by jumping up and hitting the goal, which is a bell, three metres above the ground.

Supa Punt seems at first look to be ridiculously simple. Goalies with howitzer long kicks and place kickers with a mighty hoof in rugby, would be well suited. It is one-a-side. The simple objective is to kick the ball over your opponent's goal line for a point.

Blo Ball is rather like table tennis but without bats. The idea is to blow the ball backwards and forwards. A game for people with plenty of wind!

Any of these minority sports may be coming your way. The participants take their activities extremely seriously. So, be careful if you take the mickey in your report. They will be offended, but one day they may be included in the Olympics.

There is always the temptation to stockpile the odd item or material for the silly season, just in case you run into a story shortage. This may be a newspaper or blog article, a radio interview, or a television report. In theory this is a good idea. In TV, we used to have a few spare features which we called 'shelf-items'. I once produced one about an aspiring junior athlete who had set a British record for his age group. It stayed on the shelf until it collected a layer of thick dust. The problem was by the time we got around to airing the report, the athlete was no longer a junior and had lost the record. The item had gone past its sell-by date and ended up as a piece of recycled tape.

Another factor that is more common in sport, than other forms of journalism, is people who have the habit of punctuating their conversation with exclamations of your first name. I recall interviewing a boxing promoter who would reply to a question by saying something like...

'The situation Dennis, is that my new middleweight Dennis, is set for a title chance. I have found out Dennis, that the champion will defend against him Dennis. So, Dennis, it looks like we have got a shot at the title.'

I also once interviewed an Australian rugby star who had the same familiar approach. I interviewed him after he had downed a few whiskies. Very large whiskies! He started by saying, 'well, Dennis, it's a big game'. As the interview progressed, he uttered, 'we're all looking forward to the match, Desmond.' Then at the end of the chat, 'it's been good to speak to you, Derek.' Dennis, Desmond, Derek, I was confused about my own identity. Meanwhile, he filled up another voluminous tumbler of Scotch.

Let me elucidate on two or three more of my favourite gripes. The way international football is being structured, England versus the Eddystone Lighthouse in a World Cup

Qualifier could happen! We always wait with mounting excitement for the World Cup or the European Nations' Cup; but one feature really bugs me about qualification for these tournaments.

I can just imagine that in the future, England will be facing World Cup or European Championship qualifiers against Ibiza, the Isle of Man, the Dogger Bank, Sark, or the Eddystone Lighthouse. In many ways, all the aforementioned have as good a claim to take part in the World Cup or Euros as San Marino, Andorra, and Liechtenstein. It seems that quite a few new nations have emerged over the last few decades, some with spurious claims to take part in international football tournaments. How many more 'nations' can be created? Gibraltar, with a population of around 33,000 people, is the latest spurious country to go into the hat for the draw.

I remember one of the San Marino v England matches, which was completely ludicrous. A country of about sixty million, against a 'nation' or, more accurately, an Italian hillside with 31,000 inhabitants (about the same size as Melton Mowbray, Darwen or Letchworth). The game, won 8-0 by England, was at best like watching a training exercise of attack versus defence. San Marino deployed two defensive lines of four and six virtually on the edge of their penalty area and opted for damage limitation. Their fans rapturously celebrated winning a corner as though it was a spectacular winning goal. They were lucky to get away with only shipping in eight.

It is difficult to overrun any side playing like that. If Accrington Pork Butchers Sunday team were fit and well organised and played England with ten men behind the ball and two defensive lines outside the box, they would be hard enough to break down.

It really is only a political technicality that qualifies some 'nations' in top competitions. The Isle of Man has its own parliament, an 85,000 population and has more credibility as a country than San Marino. So, the Eddystone Lighthouse could quite conceivably be set up as a separate nation as it is a long way off our shore. Matches against these 'mini-countries' really clog up tournaments. They are a bore and a waste of time. The games are pointless… and nearly always pointless for San Marino.

The authorities should set up a tiddler's qualifying competition for the likes of San Marino, Gibraltar, Liechtenstein (population 34,000), and Andorra (population 77,000). The winner of this league could then be admitted to the group stages of a major tournament. Otherwise, we could be facing a farcical situation. Just imagine a hypothetical scenario. Spain pip England to a World Cup qualifying place on goal difference because they trounced the Eddystone Lighthouse 21-0, whereas England only beat them 17-0!

I have another big sporting exasperation. You cannot beat a sizzling summer of cricket at some of our lovely county grounds, with salad lunches, cream teas, cold beers, and suntan oil. More likely, persistent rain, hot soup, umbrellas, and players holed up in the pavilion for days on end. If we do seem set for a scorcher, according to the long-range weather forecast, then all well and good. It is when the rain intervenes in one-day matches that I become really aggravated. It is all down to two words, Duckworth/Lewis.

Frank Duckworth and Tony Lewis produced a brilliant statistical plan. They devised an intricate mathematical formula to calculate the target score for the team batting second in a game interrupted by the weather. I would have preferred it if they had used their mathematical expertise to devise better train timetables or equations that calculate the distance from Pluto to Chipping Sodbury. The D/L method first appeared in 1996 and is now universally employed. It is supposed to be statistically fair, whatever that means, but it is far too complex and can easily be misunderstood. I do agree it is an award-winning, wonderful piece of academic work but better suited to the studies of mega-brained students of mathematics than first-class cricketers.

The joy and intrigue of cricket, or any sport, is the unpredictability. Duckworth/Lewis attempts to predict the unpredictable. Just think about a match like England's test win over Australia at Headingley in 1981. England was 500-1 to win at one stage. If a game is curtailed or wiped out by rain, then so be it. Go back to the old system, just award each team a limited number of points and call the game a no-result. I do not want to see a rain spoiled match with a contrived finish from a load of mathematical tables. If we must find a way of deciding the outcome of cricket games interrupted or ended by the weather, let us devise something very, very much simpler than the D/L method. Preferably just ditch it.

What I find particularly annoying is at the first hint of dark clouds or rain, players sitting on the balcony start consulting the complex D/L charts. To me, winning a match by the D/L method makes it a lottery. Imagine a football or rugby match being abandoned for some reason and the result decided by an equation. It would be ridiculous.

I would like to see the D/L method ripped up and consigned to the wheelie bin of cricket history. If a match is rained off, I would rather the outcome was decided by a pie-throwing contest or egg and spoon race. At least that would be competitive, rather than a set of calculations invented by two brilliant boffins.

To continue with the subject of cricket, there is a minor irritation that is developing into a bigger itch. It is the number of breaks in play that are now taking place in test and international matches. This is one reason why the over rate per hour has come down so much. A drink break half-way through a session is sensible enough, but there are so many other interruptions. If there is the slightest doubt about their bat, players will opt for a change. So, the game is halted by a twelfth man coming on with three or four bats for the player to choose from. They all look new and identical. There are also changes of gloves, often used as a ruse to bring out a message from the skipper. Extra drinks come on to the field, and players have more and more comfort breaks. It is sometimes impossible to keep track of who is on the field and who is off. There are also some absurdly long pauses in the action while captain, bowler and a few senior professionals form a committee to decide on-field changes. This is especially time-consuming in one-day competitions. I sometimes expect the players to sit down in a circle and bring out a whiteboard or computer to engage in deliberations.

Another slight annoyance to me is the so-called 'close season' in football. Not so long ago, the cup final was in the first week of May, and players came back for training at the beginning of July, with the league starting in the second week of August. I am a fanatical football fan, but I enjoyed the three months break from the intensity of a soccer season. It made me appreciate the game even more. There was also a bit of time to devote to cricket, tennis, athletics, rugby league and golf. As a result, to use theatrical parlance, the audience was left wanting more. After weeks and weeks without the glorious game, fans were pawing the ground, waiting for the return of their football fix.

Also, the summer sojourn gave players time to recuperate from long-term injuries and get the weariness out of their systems after a tough winter slog. For clubs there was more time to sort out business, like contracts and transfers.

But the 'close season' is closing up so fast, it is almost shut.

Now the play-offs and international tours stretch the season out until the end of May and beyond. Players return for pre-season training earlier and earlier. Most clubs report back just over halfway through June. The season also starts a week earlier. The situation also means wealthy Premiership stars get barely three weeks to create havoc at popular Mediterranean resorts!

My rant continues!

One thing that sport does better than any other form of entertainment, even showbiz, is hype; from mediocre events that are billed as earthmoving to emerging stars who are built up to be the greatest ever in their field. Sometimes to their own detriment, sport performers believe in their own puffed-up publicity. Boxing does this in spectacular style. There are now four major World Championship belts. To rate them in order of prestige they would be the WBC, WBA, IBF and WBO. It is a pity there are four and not one belt, but all these titles are credible. Over the last twenty years, lots of other world championship belts have been created; some have not lasted long. These are blown up as big titles but are really non-events and very confusing.

Another more amusing part of boxing hype is some of the fictional promotions of fighters on a bill. I remember an American being brought over to England some time ago as 'an opponent' for a leading British heavyweight. It turned out the fighter was a lumberjack from Texas who was engaging in his first professional contest. On the posters he was heralded as 'The Champion of Texas'. In tune with his occupation, he was chopped down like a big tree.

At one time, every contemporary folk singer with a few interesting lines or verses was titled, 'the new Bob Dylan'. It was similar in cricket, as every time England produced a promising all-rounder, the press would be hailing him as 'the new Ian

Botham'. Botham was extraordinary and unique, the only player to compare with him is Ben Stokes; but to me, they are different players and not to be measured against each other. It is the same in many sports... 'the new George Best', 'the new Nijinsky' or the new 'Senna'. I have lost count of the number of footballers who have been dubbed, 'the new Messi'. Most of these seem to have faded from view. What is not in doubt is there could never be a 'new Garry Sobers' or 'new Muhammad Ali'.

Horses can also be 'over-hyped'. I remember a few certs to win the Derby or Gold Cup that failed to make out. One I particularly recall was Gorytus. Several friends who were racing journalists told me he was going to be a wonder horse, and these were correspondents with a great deal of expertise and many years of experience on the turf. When he ran as a two-year-old in 1982, I was told to get my money down and back him for the next year's Derby. Gorytus seemed to have everything going for him. He was sired by the great Nijinsky. His dam, Glad Rags, won the 1000 Guineas in 1966. The horse was bred in Virginia and sent over to England to be trained by the excellent Dick Hern and ridden by one of the greatest jockeys of all time, Willie Carson.

In his first two races, Gorytus more than fulfilled the hype. He won the Acomb Stakes at York, as Carson guided him home to win by an impressive seven lengths. His winning time broke the track record by over a second. An extraordinary debut. A month later he was back on track. The race was the group two Champagne Stakes at Doncaster over seven furlongs. Gorytus started as odds-on favourite in a class field. Despite that, he eased away over the final two furlongs to win by five lengths. Willie Carson did not even have to use the whip.

He was now headed for the 2000 Guineas and The Derby in 1983. Even at this stage, the bookmakers made him 4-1 favourite for the Guineas and 5-1 favourite for the Derby, despite the fact the races were a year away. I remember backing the wonder horse as my racing reporter pals seemed to be spot on in their assessment.

Gorytus had one more race that season, at Newmarket in the Dewhurst Stakes. He was the 1/2 favourite in a strong field, but around the halfway mark, Gorytus started to struggle and came home last, thirty lengths adrift. All sorts of theories were put forward as to why the horse had performed so badly. Was he sick? Did he suffer from a breathing problem? Was he doped? Some of the stories were a bit far-fetched. The stable reported that he seemed distressed but recovered very quickly. By the time of the 2000 Guineas, Gorytus looked to be in great shape again, but after a good start faded to finish fifth. It was felt he would not relish the soft going for The Derby and failed to be placed in two more races. It was a great shame that he did not live up to the hype of the wonder horse after his first two races. We will probably never know why.

It is not only horses that can get hyped up. Greyhound racing provides an enjoyable, fun night out. I have little knowledge of the sport, and I do not think I have ever made a penny after a dabble with the dogs. But one night I thought my luck was going to change. A contact I had who was a track owner, informed me that a dog running in his next meeting was going to be a sensation. Was this going to be the next Mick the Miller or Ballyregan Bob? The greyhound had certainly travelled a long way to take part in the meeting, which I thought was a good sign. He was also a red-hot favourite. This was going to be a formality, and I would beat my dog racing jinx. But before the race, he quite literally had the runs. Not quite such a good sign. The animal fell rather than flew out of the traps and ambled round to finish a distant last. Better luck next time!

My final tirade is not so much a groan or grouse but sheer grief. At one time athletics was close to being my favourite sport, especially when Olympics and World Championships came around. It is such a natural event. What is more instinctive than running, jumping and throwing? The Rome Olympics in 1960, the first to be comprehensively televised, vied in excitement with the 1958 Football World Cup in Sweden and the emergence of Pele.

But my fervour for track and field has faded over the years, owing to the increased influence of drugs. I want to watch a fair contest, not a chemistry competition, where athletes have the edge over an opponent, thanks to the dope and medication they have been imbibing, infusing, or injecting. If we take as an example the sprint events, there is a long list of competitors who have failed dope tests. This includes many big names in the sport and former champions and record holders.

In many of the field events, the consumption of anabolic steroids has been flagrant. These drugs have been swallowed like smarties by those in disciplines like the shot-put, hammer and discus. Again, the list of offenders is very lengthy.

Prior to the crumbling of the iron curtain, some Eastern European countries instituted national doping programmes for athletes. Reams of documentary evidence have been unearthed from the former East Germany or DDR. In October 1985, Marita Koch of East Germany set a world record for the women's four hundred metres of 47.60 seconds. The mark was quite simply extraordinary, so much so that at the time of writing, no other woman has come close. The only other runner to duck under 48 seconds and by just a hundredth of a second was Jarmila Kratochvilova of Czechoslovakia, another nation with a well-documented doping programme for athletes. Kratochvilova set the women's world eight hundred metres record of 1 minute 53.28 seconds back in 1983. A record not surpassed by 2020.

It must be stressed that neither Koch or Kratochvilova ever failed a drug test, and both athletes insist they never used performance-enhancing substances. With standards of knowledge, training, diet and fitness constantly improving and evolving it would seem odd that no runner has come close to the records of Koch and Kratochvilova set in 1985 and 1983 respectively. Documents obtained from former East German research programmes list dosage and timetables for administration of anabolic steroids to many athletes, including Marita Koch. It would be good to know that these athletes are completely innocent of illegal drug usage, but we will never know.

Drug taking has become more sophisticated in sport and especially in track and field. Masking agents have been used to cover up traces of performance-enhancing drugs. The scientists and chemists often stay a step ahead of the drug policing bodies. So, I would like to see an extremely rigid screening process before all major championships to weed out and banish the drug cheats.

Nowadays, when I am watching athletics, I find myself a little distracted. As the runners line up, I am pondering which ones are cheats and which ones are clean. At times I wonder what I am really looking at. I have often enjoyed the performance of a top performer and then been disappointed to find out they are a drug cheat. What was once a noble activity has been thoroughly tarnished over the years, and for me the sheer enjoyment has been diminished.

One of my least favourite clichés which particularly relates to football is, 'it's a squad game !' Managers rattle on about squad rotation, using the bench and tactical tweaks these days. There is no doubt that football is now an eighteen-man game, with the liberal use of substitutions and, to be fair, all the better for it.

So, I fondly recall a college football team I played in. We barely had eleven players, let alone a squad. It is true to say we could field a reasonable, basic eleven, but outside that, we had little to spare, in fact, one man in reserve. We did trawl the University to beef up the squad but to no avail.

Our only goalie was a little hesitant but very spectacular. He seemed to make late decisions. We discovered the reason he pawed or palmed the ball away at the last possible moment was because he was extremely short-sighted. In fact, he could only see the ball when it was a few feet in front of his face. Off the pitch, he wore bottle bottom glasses. With perfect eyesight, he would have been a pro.

We had just one stand-in player if one of our 'eleven' dropped out. He was a 'fresh-faced young fresher' called Kev. The way things worked out, he always got a game, as we predictably lost a student from the side due to injury or absence during the week. Kev was not so much a utility player as an utterly useless player.

He was one of those characters who played up to what I call, 'inverted modesty'. Whenever he was required to make up the numbers, he would trawl for compliments by saying something like, 'bad luck, lads, I'm playing, that will seriously weaken the side.' Then one of the team would foolishly reply, 'no, it won't Kev, you're a good player.' Or he would make a comment like, 'pity you could not get anyone else.' And again, one of the team would pander to his plea for a pat on the back, 'don't worry, Kev, you always give one hundred per cent.'

This scenario went on for a full season. Every time we

thought we had every member of our best eleven fit and ready, someone would drop out with a bug or strain, and Kev would make up the number. It was really infuriating.

It was the last match of the season, and Kev snuck into the side after a last-minute casualty. Once again, in the dressing room, he tried to prompt a little praise by saying, 'bad luck, lads, I'm in the team.' And our captain replied, 'yes, it's terrible luck 'cos you're fucking useless, Kev.' He was gobsmacked. Marvellous! That took the words out of my mouth. I had wanted to say that all season. Anyway, it is a squad game!

I mentioned earlier how the economic muscle of football had changed the players' status and wealth in the modern game. Whenever sport "journos" get together, they tend to compare and compile various factors. On one occasion, while waiting around for something to happen at a soccer club, we came up with a list of the ten things you always find at a top footballer's house. This was brought about as I had visited a club captain at his new home, which ticked every box for a footballer's domain.

The guidelines were:

It is often the show home on a new estate.

There is always a Bentley, Merc or Range Rover poking out of the garage.

A blonde wife who is a former model or beautician.

A big dog.

Huge settees or sofas made of leather or covered in animal prints.

A massive TV with DVDs strewn around it.

Pictures of the player with trophies and cups in the hall and downstairs loo.

The thickest pile carpets.

A bar in the corner with optics.

A snooker or pool table.

Once again, this is a major generalisation and exaggeration. Of course, it could be interpreted there is more than a hint of jealousy when observing a Premiership star's wealth.

As you get older, one sporting club to avoid is the 'back in my day' brigade. Never get into this habit! It is a very condescending attitude. People saying that everything was better when they were younger. Seeing they are still alive, what the hell was 'my day'. The way I look at life, my day is now! What these people go on to claim is sport and life were better years ago. It is not. Standard of life and medical care are getting better all the time. Life expectancy is rising.

In sport, the 'back in my day' braggarts will say that everything was faster, stronger, more skilful and better in every way. What they have failed to notice is, most sports are improving and progressing every year. That is backed up in a lot of activities by statistics, times, measurements, and film footage.

If you look at old pictures of football matches from another era, you will notice that players are much fitter now and have more muscular physiques. They are more complete athletes. Today's pitches are like bowling greens, so the ball can be zipped around at pace. Techniques have been enhanced. The game is played at a much faster tempo, and passing is more accurate. Tactics have also improved and become much more sophisticated, which is due in no small measure to top foreign coaches at the helm of many of our clubs.

I would also point out the huge improvements to stadia. Even in the lower divisions, there are good seats, stands that do not leak like a cabbage strainer and food and beverages at half time. There is also a revolution in facilities, with state-of-the-art training grounds that have medical centres, gyms, canteens and swimming pools. One factor I do miss from football a few decades ago are full-blooded, bone-shaking tackles. There were some great defenders like Norman Hunter and Tommy Smith who could certainly win a meaty clash, but I must agree that ruling out the tackle from behind, gnashing studs-first lunges and other dangerous challenges, has vastly improved the skill levels and aided the more talented players.

'Back in my day', footballers with knee cartilage injuries, cruciate ligament tears and some more simple problems would have faced the end of their careers. Now medicine and surgery can work modern miracles. As I have mentioned, football was played on pitches like a quagmire, with workman's boots and balls that weighed as much as my great aunt Florence's suet puddings. Some of the so-called 'stadiums' were disgusting amalgams of rotting wood and rusting metal. At Watford, we stood on a bank of slurry in one corner. Toilets were revolting. There was a big blockhouse-gents on one corner and no facilities for ladies. Apart from the Bovril and those famous roasted peanuts at some top grounds, catering was not seen as important.

God knows what was in the middle of some 1950s pies. Now, most grounds are family-friendly.

In cricket, one-day fixtures have radically improved skills, but the 'in my day' cult would tell us that bowlers were faster, batsmen were better. I am not a great fan of twenty 20, but this form of the game has sharpened up fielding skills, enhanced the athleticism of the players, led to faster scoring rates and added a few more shots to the batsman's repertoire. It is now common to see reverse sweeps played in test matches. To add to the debate, difficult slip catches in days of yore are now standard. We now have a great deal more international cricket to watch across three different formats. Rugby union is unrecognisable since professionalism in 1995 and completely different from the game of fifty or sixty years ago. The most obvious change is the size and power in every position. I remember top club games in the sixties and seventies that were a complete bore. That was before the direct kick to touch was outlawed. In these encounters, the half backs often tried to inch upfield by kicking for touch at every opportunity. There was also the forward pile-up, like a pyramid of bodies, slowing the game to a standstill. It could be a long time before the ball emerged.

As for tennis, you only have to look at old films of past champions and compare them with the top stars of today. The modern players are fitter, hit the ball harder and are more accurate. This is just natural development in tactics, training and techniques. Also, the fact that rackets are so much better. Sport can only improve. Federer, Nadal, and Djokovic are arguably the three greatest players of all time in the men's game. That is backed up by statistics as they have won more grand slam events than any other players. In twenty, or thirty years' time, we will be talking about a trio of players who are even better. This will be proven by comparing pictures. The next generation of stars will probably hit the ball even harder and more accurately, have adapted new shots and use hi-tech rackets.

A day at the races or evening at the dogs is now much more of a social occasion. Grandstands have improved, and the venues are now more conducive to corporate entertainment or family outings. At many racing venues, the catering is first class. Even dogs and horses have much more advanced training programmes, veterinary care and diets.

In athletics, most times and distances are gradually improving, except in a few unique instances I mentioned earlier. In the Rome Olympics in 1960, Otis Davies of the United States set a world record of 44.9 seconds to become the first man to break forty-five seconds for the four hundred metres. Fifty-six years later, South African Wayde Van Niekerk clocked an incredible 43.03, nearly two seconds faster.

In the Pole Vault, Don Bragg of the USA set a world mark of 4.80 metres in 1960. Sergey Bubka of the Soviet Union, one of the greatest athletes of all time, continually improved the record to reach 6.14 metres in 1994. Armand Duplantis of Sweden stretched the height to 6.18 metres in 2020. So even records held by the greatest stars in athletics history eventually get overhauled.

The mile world record is an interesting case. When Roger Bannister ducked under four minutes for the event at Oxford in 1956, recording a time of 3 minutes 59.4 seconds, it was heralded quite rightly as superhuman. Now it is a rarely run distance, but in 1999 Hicham El Guerrouj of Morocco set a world record of 3 minutes 43.13 seconds.

To show progression in another sport, we can compare the times for the winners in flat racing's blue riband event, the Epsom Derby. We do have to bear in mind that the Derby can be raced in all sorts of conditions. A race in a quagmire this year would be slower than a trip on firm or good going fifty years ago. Here are a selection of Derby winners and times:

1900 Diamond Jubilee – 2 minutes 42 seconds.

1935 Bahram – 2 minutes 36 seconds.

1970 Nijinsky – 2 minutes 34.68 seconds.

2010 Workforce – 2 minutes 31.33 seconds.

This information shows an extraordinary progression. As the Derby distance is fractionally over one and a half miles, an improvement of over ten and a half seconds is a long way.

I do get the fact that great stars from another era, whether a horse like Diamond Jubilee, a footballer like Tom Finney or tennis player like Jean Borotra would still be great in the modern day. They were born with extraordinary talent and would have been even better with today's training, equipment and diets.

But of course, things were better in my day. We had lice, nits, scabies and roundworm. There were still killer diseases like TB, Polio and Typhoid. In some cities, thick yellow smog exacerbated conditions like asthma and bronchitis. In many factories, mines and workplaces, conditions were dreadful and often dangerous. Foreign holidays were a dream, except for those who were comfortably off. Television was restricted to just four channels just over twenty years ago. For those old enough to remember, a few years further back, we had rationing. There were a few positives like spam, corned beef, broken biscuits, tripe, beef dripping and vesta curries. The 1950s and early '60s were austere times, and the country was still recovering economically from the horrors of the Second World War, but the playing or watching of sport was probably the greatest release from the rigours of rationing, recession, and reconstruction. As the decades have continued into the twenty-first century, we now have many more forms of sport, recreation and pastimes to enjoy.

One of the advantages of sport reporting is you very rarely get involved in dangerous situations or sent to world trouble spots, except perhaps Millwall. However, some cities on a Saturday night could come into this category.

As part of coverage of the 1996 European Nations Football Championship, I contributed to a series about the effects of soccer hooliganism in different countries. Turkey was among the nations taking part. I was sent to report on the clash between supporters of Galatasaray and Fenerbahce in Istanbul, a hostile derby. So much so that supporters of the losing side tend to hide away the next day and not come out in public.

Our introduction to the fun was one group of fans running up the road and hurling bricks and lumps of concrete at the opposition supporters. The camera crew and I took shelter sitting on a water cannon. By this time, police and troops were involved in quelling the fracas. To my surprise, they were quite amused by the masonry throwing contest. They laughed and said to us something along the lines of. 'It's just the lads having fun.' Being hit by a brick was not my idea of amusement, but after the game we heard handguns being fired into the air by jubilant supporters. I am relieved to say this practice does not happen in Istanbul any more but give me a summer day and a cricket match at Lords with tea and cucumber sandwiches anytime!

Epilogue

As that great bard and philosopher Bruce Springsteen once said – *'You can't light a fire without a spark'* – and those few words expertly sum up what is needed to take the first step to becoming a sport writer or broadcaster. You need a vital spark to ignite that intense passion. To be a sport reporter, you have got to be obsessed with the subject. Mad for it. Completely obsessed! Or suffer from CSD (Compulsive Sport Disorder).

Smell the sweat.
Scent the liniment.
Feel the impact, and taste the blood.
That WOW Factor

SMELL THE SWEAT
SMELL THE LINIMENT
FEEL THE IMPACT
AND TASTE
THE BLOOD
THE WOW
FACTOR

A Homage to Heroes

The Little Master and Master Blaster,
Golden Bear, Tiger and Raging Bull,
Little Mo and Smokin' Joe,
Sugar Ray and Cassius Clay,
Iron Mike and Homicide Hank,
Sir Garfield, Sir Gareth and Sir Gordon.
Rossi, Messi and Dessie,
Fiery Fred and Lord Ted,
Fangio, Ronaldo and Faldo,
McEnroe, McCoy and McCaw,
Rummy, Rory and Beefy,
Hurricane, Whirlwind and Rocket,
Psycho, Razor and Chopper,
Chariots Offiah and Sir Ivor,
Shergar and Kauto Star,
Whispering Death and Lightning Bolt,
Di Stefano, Puskas and Gento,
Edson Arantes Do Nascimento.